WORTH
OF
WORTHLESS
MEN
ADUANYA IFEANYI DAVID

THE

WORTH

OF

WORTHLESS MEN

(Power Of Insignificant Things)

ADUANYA IFEANYICHUKWU DAVID

TABLE OF CONTENTS

INTRODUCTION

I have come across so many persons who think for one reason or the other that life is unfair or God was unfair at creation. People who have looked at their lives and actually got to believe that there is nothing good about them. They get to blame their parents, blame the government, blame the church, and blame the society for how they believe their lives have turned out.

No man did God ever create without a definite purpose with what He desires to do with such a man. No man is product of coincidence and no one is a mistake. Our God is a God of order and nothing happens without His knowledge and hence, the fact that you are alive is clear indication that there is something awesome about you.

""Before I made you in your mother's womb, I knew you. Before you were born, I chose you for a special work. I chose you to be a prophet to the nations." – Jeremiah 1:5. (ERV)

This scripture gives us a clear picture of what God does with every man. No one was ever formed in the belly that he didn't know of and no one was ever released from the womb without an assignment.

To Jeremiah He assigned to be a prophet unto nations, to some he has assigned to be pastors to tend his flock, to some He assigned to be musicians to sing His praise to nations, to others he gave one assignment or the other just for His glory. There is a special task assigned for you. You have a special place in Gods agenda.

But how unfortunate that so many have allowed others opinion to define the path of their lives and destinies. So many have allowed their lives to be shaped by what others think of them. No wonder apostle Paul recognizing this, spoke to timothy and said, let no one despise thy youth.

"Do not let anyone look down on you because you are young..." – 1 Timothy 4:12 (ISV)

Let no one look down on you, have an idea of who you are, know who God calls you. Many have looked down on themselves because men talked down on them.

Have you lost your self-confidence because of past experiences? Have you bowed your head in shame and shrink yourself in a cage just because someone talked down on you?

Have you been told, there is nothing good about you just like Nathaniel spoke about Nazareth "can any good thing come out of Nazareth?" (John 1:46) and you are now thinking, maybe they are right after all, maybe there is actually nothing good about me, have you tried so many things and it looked like nothing is working out right and you are thinking you cannot get anything right?

I have good news for you. God has not looked down on you and in you He sees great treasure. There is something great you carry, men may not see it but the Lord knows of it. Others may disregard it, but the Lord wants to use it to set you on high.

Don't count yourself off yet. There is great worth in you, there is big treasure waiting to be put to use. It is time to gird up your loins and move again. It is never over until God says it is over and it can never be over until you have fulfilled purpose.

CHAPTER ONE

NOTHING LACKS WORTH

CHAPTER ONE

NOTHING LACKS WORTH

Everything God created was never without a reason or purpose. The plants, the animals, the rocks, the seas, the sky, every single thing that popped out at creation was for a reason.

The colours in flowers, the hairs on animals, even the abstract things of life has an assignment. I came to discover that certain insects don't see certain colours, so next time you pass through a beautiful flower and wowed by its colours, just remember those colours in flowers are also there for a purpose.

They also have an assignment of attracting certain insects for its pollination, wow. If those colours weren't there, those flowers will not get pollinated. The plants supplying the oxygen needed by animals and in turn the animals supplying the carbon dioxide needed by these plants. Everything divinely planned out with nothing left out in His agenda.

Likewise there is no man that was created without a purpose, there is no one that ever came out of the womb without a life assignment. Every man has a destiny to fulfill and your destiny already is a thing of great value.

Even before your parents thought of your conception, God had you in mind. He has planned out your life and he carefully created you to fit into His divine plan for your life.

The bible says your life matters because God uniquely designed you.

Psalms 139:13-16 – "For you created every part of me, you put me together in my mother's womb.

> *vs15. When my bones were being formed, carefully put together in my mother's womb, when I was growing there in secret, you knew that I was there.*
>
> *vs16. You saw me before I was born, the days allotted to me had all been recorded in your book, before any of them began." (GNV)*

God made you uniquely because he has a unique plan for your life. He personally oversaw your creation, carefully designed your height, your complexion, be you fair or dark, your stature, your size and everything because he had something for you to do that only you can do.

Nothing in your life is out of place. I have seen many brooding over one thing or the other about their physical appearance but forgetting that, it was the same appearance that God looked upon after creation and said it was good. If God in his infinite wisdom and beauty says I look good the way I am, I wonder which devil would come to make me feel bad about my appearance. Your parents may not have planned it out but God did.

God has set everyone apart for a special use. You are not an accident, you have great value because you were designed in God's image, he planned your life before you were born, and you were made for his pleasure.

THE BIG ISSUE OF WORTHLESSNESS

> *"But some Jews gathered WORTHLESS LOAFERS from the streets and formed a mob. They set the whole city in uproar..." – Acts 17:5 (GNV)*

Reading this verse of the scripture, it bothered me why the bible would choose to call people created in the image of God worthless. Funny enough, I was wondering if the bible was actually being rude or disrespectful to the image of God, but the definite answer is NO, all scriptures are inspired of the Spirit.

No one word, or sentence in the scriptures is meaningless or a mistake, all were well articulated and inspired by the spirit hence if the scriptures said its so, then it is so.

Having learnt to take the bible by its word, as I remembered having an issue when God called a man a fool in the bible,

---

"But God said to him, thou fool, this night thy soul shall be required of thee: then whose shall these things be, which thou hast provided" – Luke 12:20 (KJV)

Knowing God forbids us from calling our brothers fools or else be in danger of hell, as we see in Mathew 5:22

"… but whosoever shall say to his brother, thou fool, shall be in danger of hell" – Mathew 5:22. (KJV)

It also bothered me why God would call His own creation a fool. It seemed to me like a father calling his own son a 'bastard' but then it is written, "A fool says in his heart that there is no God" – psalms 14:1.

Only a fool would say "There is no God!" people like that are worthless… – Psalm 14:1 (CEV)

The decisions and directions we choose can either make us worth full or make us worthless, little wonder God called the greedy farmer in Luke 12:20 a fool, because his thoughts and decisions were filled with self and not with God. The man in question certainly had no regard for God and hence there is no two ways about it, he was actually a fool.

In the same vein, the men in Acts 17:5 had no kingdom interest, which was why they became furious at the conversions (kingdom project) made by Paul and Silas in Thessalonica. Thus making themselves vessels unto dishonour by virtue of the dishonourable things they did. Such I knew the scriptures was not exaggerating by using the word "worthless".

A search of the same scripture from other translations further reveals to us the nature of these men.

"But the Jews which believed not, moved with envy, took unto them certain LEWD fellows of the baser sort..." Acts 17:5 (KJV)

"But the Jews were jealous, so they rounded up some BAD CHARACTER from the market place..." (NIV)

"But the Jews became jealous and with the help of some RUFFIANS in the market places..." (RSV)

Some other translations used the word vile, evil men, etc.

LEWD meaning to be Lascivious, sexually promiscuous, rude, uneducated, vulgar, common, vile etc.

RUFFIANS which means to be a scoundrel, rascal or unprincipled, deceitful, brutal and unreliable persons.

With these, there is no doubt, the scripture was not exaggerating on the word worthless. Of a truth, these men had no value to the society, as the bible clearly exposed their lifestyle and their character, no one should actually want to have anything to do with them judging from their personality.

WHICH EVER WAY, YOU ARE WANTED

I must emphatically say that there is no man, no woman, no child, no boy or girl that is useless. Every single person in this world is useful and still every single thing in this world is useful because everything you can see was made for a specific purpose. There is great worth in every man, but the usability actually depends on who is using the man.

Your usefulness is relative to whom you are useful to. Just like the saying, *one man's food is another's poison*, you cannot serve two opposing masters.

Hence it seems that there is always a war over the lives of everyone, a war of dominion and ownership of a man's destiny but it actually lies in the hands of the man to choose who to crown winner. One cannot possibly crown two opponents winners in this race. There is a need for decision.

"No man can serve two masters; for either he will hate one and love the other, or else he will hold to the one and despise the other. Ye cannot serve God and mammon" – Mathew 6:24 (KJV)

You cannot be fulfilling Gods mandate and as well as serve the devils purposes. If you cannot please God, then certainly you are a great pleasure to the devil, an awful comic show.

If God cannot use you, the devil would, definitely. In whichever way, somebody is declaring you WANTED! You are still needed for what you carry. Just as the popular saying "*The enemy of my enemy is my friend*".

This was the exact case of the men aforementioned in Acts 17:5, they weren't needed in the society but their worth was discovered by the jealousy of the Jews. They were good for nothing, but for the purpose of causing an unholy uproar, they were the most qualified for the job and all over the society. No matter how bad your life seems to be, someone still needs you.

IT'S MY LIFE

It pains my heart to see destinies, the devil is wasting. Of course so many of them started out in the church and I wondered what the devil really showed them, that could replace the great worth and value the Lord had placed on them. Was the price actually worth the treasure?

Youthful but not useful to the Kingdom. I have heard so many youths say *"I have just one life to live so let me live it to the fullest"*, so many others fool themselves to think *"it is my life, let me live it the way I want"* and I only weep at how much the devil has blinded them.

Yea you may be right, it is your life after all but know that, no man is a master of his own destiny. There is a war for mastery over that destiny, there is a war for control over that life and only you can choose which way to go.

> ***"Lord, I know that no one is a master of his own destiny; no person has control over his own life" – Jeremiah 10:23***

And for what God intends to make out of your life, He is always calling out, that you end this war now and choose Him. The destination of a ship is determined by the captain, he would choose where to head the ship.

There are so many vessels meant for great works, vessels of great worth, who but for the pleasure of this life, have sold out their worth. They have sold out their treasure just as Esau sold out his birthright for a pottage, and hence lost their worth in the presence of our God, no wonder scriptures call them worthless.

IN HIM WAS LIFE

Maybe it will interest you to know that loss of Gods personality and nature is loss of value (worth). Life really makes no meaning outside God. The loss of value (worth) is loss of purpose and the loss of purpose is simply a life unlived.

The totality of a meaningful life revolves round the person of Jesus. I doubt if my life would ever have made sense without Him.

God says we are the light of the world, but interestingly, we have no light of our own, the light men see is nothing but the life of Jesus. Hence there would be no light shining out of our lives, if we distance myself from the source of the light, and the life of Jesus is gradually being untangled from our own lives.

---

*"In Him was life and the life was
the light of men" (KJV)*

*"The word was the source of life and this life
brought light to humanity" – John 1:4 (GNV)*

Just like the revolution of the planets round the sun, each time a particular side gets close to the sun, it receives light and we call it day break, and the closer it gets, the more light we see when we say day time or noon and as soon as it starts distancing itself from the sun, the light received goes down and its evening and the farther it goes from the source, the darker it becomes and we experience night.

In the same vein, God is the source of our light, and His life we live is our light to the world. The closer we come to him, the brighter our light shines to His glory and the farther we go from Him, the dimmer our lights become till there is no more light to shine.

I remember when I started distancing myself from God, started postponing prayer times even when God was pressing it hard on me, I could barely sit to study my bible, I was actually losing my relationship as it was just standing on a thin wire, got so busy actually doing nothing and I was losing saltiness, I was losing value.

"But this precious treasure – this light and power that now shine within us- is held in perishable containers, that is, in our weak bodies. So everyone can see that our glorious power is from God and is not our own." – 2 Corinthians 4:7-8. (NLT)

In the same manner, we are the salt of the world, but the only taste we can add to this world is the life of Christ, as without it, we are actually unsalted. And that makes me want to rephrase the aforementioned scripture and say "in Him was life and the life was the taste of the world".

CREATED FOR HIS PLEASURE:

"Thou are worthy, O Lord, to receive glory and honour and power for thou hast created all things and for thy pleasure they are and were created" – Revelation 4:11 (KJV)

No manufacturer ever produces a thing for the purpose of bringing him pain and dissatisfaction, and God in all His creation, did so that His creation may bring Him pleasure. That was why He had to look back at it after creating and it pleased Him to see that it was good.

It is so heartwarming that God looks at me and calls me good. Scriptures say we were beautifully and wonderfully made, created in the image and excellency of our king and maker. But every soul living outside His will and purposes does not give Him pleasure.

I hate the thoughts of being alive and not serving the purpose of my maker, or live a life in which He cannot derive pleasure from. I sincerely see it as living a worthless life.

If I was created for His pleasure, then the totality of my life should fulfill that as anything away from it means I make null and void the purpose of my creation.

Imagine having a dress that doesn't fit anymore. No matter how much you love the dress and how precious it may be to you, you will certainly have to dispose it or give it away someday.

God loves us so very much, such that He gave His only son to die for us even while we were yet sinners. He never wants to see any of His children lost but the issue is that, the more He looks at us without any pleasure, and as He does all HE can do to bring us to light, He does it knowing that a time is coming when He cannot help it but take a decision. There is a period of grace.

THERE IS AN EXPECTATION ON YOU

*"Every branch in me that beareth not fruit
he taketh away and every branch that
beareth fruit, he purgeth it, that it may bring
forth more fruit" – John 15:2 (KJV)*

Every branch is intended to bear fruits but the bible says that Every branch that beareth not fruit, He taketh away, telling us that He has no need for branches that bears no fruit. There is truly worthlessness when we are not fulfilling the purpose for which we were made.

God has no need for creatures that doesn't give Him pleasure but like a branch, he will always prune us, and tend for us to see if we can bear fruits but then there would be that time when He can only but cut the branch off.

Do you remember the fig tree Jesus met at Bethany when he was hungry and expected to get fruits from it but unfortunately the fig tree had no fruits?

Mark 11:12-14 – "The next day, as they were coming back from Bethany, Jesus was hungry. He saw in a distance a fig tree covered with leaves, so he went to see if he could find any figs on it. But when he came to it, he found only leaves, because it was not the right time for figs.

Jesus said to the fig tree, "No man shall ever eat figs from you again!" and his disciples heard him" (GNB)

There was an expectation on that fig tree which it did not fulfill, the master was hungry and needed something to eat. Well should I blame the fig tree as it was not even the time for figs? But yet that fig tree received a curse for not bearing fruit. How much more us?

Can I let you know that there is an expectation over your life which you must fulfill?

God expects profit from your life. Remember the parable of the ten talents, the answer which was given to the servant who refused to invest his talent makes me understand, that unproductivity is not allowed in the kingdom. Every soul not profiting the king is useless to him, and he has no need for such.

As for this useless servant – throw him outside in the dark; there he will cry and grind his teeth" – Mathew 25:30 (GNB)

Our purpose is to be a source of pleasure to our King. I doubt what excuse we can give if we don't fulfill that. We need to sincerely ask ourselves, Can the Lord get what He desires when He comes to you? Can He find pleasure when He looks in the direction of your life?

Oh!! I sincerely don't want to live my life fulfilling the devil's agenda. No man is a master of his life, it is either Jesus is at the head of my life or the enemy is.

It will really a big shame for me to live physically but dead in the spirit, shame on me, to be seen as successful, important or well doing, when heaven sees me as a worthless soul with no kingdom value. Celebrated on earth and despised in heaven. And that is why we must wake up now and strengthen what we still have before it dies completely.

The Lord is seeking for vessels, He can use to cause a holy uproar in all the nations of the world. The Lord is in search of men who would surrender their lives for His holy purpose.

I feel like pausing here to ask you beloved, how does heaven see you? Can it be said that you have a reputation of being alive but actually you are dead?

Can it be that you are highly celebrated while heaven is weeping over your soul?

That you are known to be great and fulfilled here on earth while heaven looks at you and tags you "worthless"? Can it be said that you are fulfilling the purpose of your creation which is to give ELOHIM pleasure

"I know that you have reputation of being alive, even though you are dead! So wake up, and strengthen what you still have before it dies completely"– Revelation 3:1-2

God is saying "I know you son, I know you daughter, strengthen what you still have, before it dies off completely", you must awake now to the consciousness of your life assignment, you must awake now to the consciousness of your divine calling and purpose to fulfill it.

NOW IS THE TIME

Let me also quickly remind us, just as I have stated before that there is an expectation over our lives and if we are still living our lives like we own it, without recognizing it was given to us for a purpose, then I am so sorry to say that we place our lives on a very risky stand, as the bible clearly tells us what the Lord will do with such lives.

"Also, the kingdom of heaven is like this. Some fishermen throw their net out in the lake and catch all kinds of fish. When the net is full, they pull it to shore and sit down to divide the fish: the good ones go into their buckets, the worthless ones are thrown away. It will be like this at the end of age: …"-Mathew 13:47. (GNB)

There is this saying that *"there are two people you can never lie to and they are God and yourself"*.

I may not tell where you belong, be it the good which the angels will harvest for the Lord or the worthless that will be thrown into the fiery furnace, but sure you know yourself more than anyone else.

"He spake also a parable; A certain man had a fig tree planted in his vineyard; and he came and sought fruit thereon, and found none. Then said he unto the dresser of his vineyard, behold, these three years I come seeking fruit on this fig tree, and find none: cut it down; why cumbereth it the ground? And he answering said unto him, Lord, let it alone this year also, till I shall dig about it, and dung it: And if it bear fruit, well: and if not, then after that thou shalt cut it down" – Luke 13:6-9 (KJV)

Let us imagine the Lord as the land owner, Jesus as the dresser, whereas we are the fig tree. And daily has the Lord sought to derive pleasure from our lives while Jesus stands as our great intercessor, interceding on our behalf that we may be given more time just for us to turn from our ways and come back to our maker.

Beloved how much longer would we keep the Lord seeking for pleasure in our lives?

As the owner of the vineyard comes to cut down the fig tree, yet the dresser keeps pleading on its behalf, to be given more time. How much time we have been given already tells us of the tender mercies of God towards us.

Imagine how many years we have spent already and in all these years it has been God giving us one new day to another as Jesus pleads our cause. There is nothing God would not do coming after us. There is no wall he won't kick down, no lie he won't tear down coming after us. There is no shadow He won't light up, no mountain He won't climb up just coming after us. His love is simply overwhelming and never-ending.

It is a truth worthy of note, that we are still alive is God giving us another chance to be saved.

"Look on our Lord's patience as the opportunity he is giving you to be saved..." – 2 Peter 3:15 (GNB)

As God helps us to see about this issue of worthlessness and deal with it, it is very much expedient that if you haven't made that big decision yet of handing over the control of your life to Jesus, then NOW is the time. The time is NOW that you return to your father just like the prodigal son did.

"At last he came to his senses and said..., I will get up and go to my father and say, Father, I have sinned against God and against you." – Luke 15:17 (GNB)

The devil can only take you far away from your father, strip you of your worth, and abandon you just like the prodigal son. And Jesus is calling you right now to come back to your senses because He loves you, He doesn't want to cut you down or throw you out, rather He wants you to fulfill purpose that the Lord might find pleasure in you.

Let's not procrastinate it any longer. You can bow your head at this moment and talk to your father in heaven. Scriptures says that if we believe in our hearts and confess with our mouth that Jesus is lord, then we would be saved.

So you will be saved, if you honestly say, "Jesus is Lord," and if you believe with all your heart that God raised him from death – Romans 10:9 (GNB)

If you just made that decision, then congratulations. Let's resume our ride as the Lord helps us to turn every iota of worthlessness in our lives into great worth

CHAPTER TWO

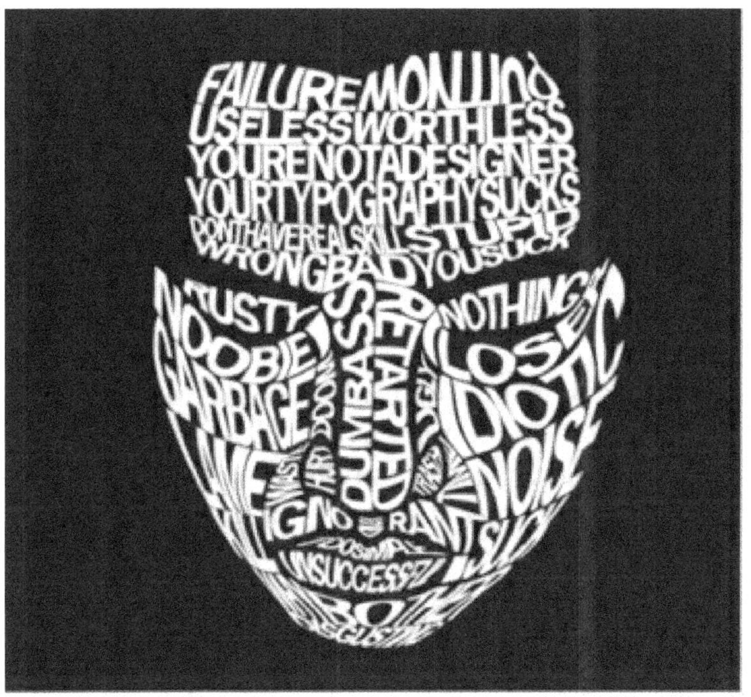

Worthless – Ignorance Of Self

CHAPTER TWO

WORTHLESS – IGNORANCE OF SELF

One of the greatest discoveries a man can ever make is the discovery of self. Pastor Myles Munroe in one of his messages said *"the greatest tragedy of life is not death, rather the greatest tragedy of life is life – life without a purpose"* He continued to say that *"nothing is worse than being alive without knowing why you are alive"*.

Then I thought to myself, is there actually a life without purpose as every single thing God made was for a definite purpose? And then I was convinced, of a truth one of the greatest tragedies of life is a life with an undiscovered purpose.

Certainly everyone has a purpose, but not everyone has discovered their purpose and certainly not everyone ever will.

So many people roaming the streets today with no slight idea of why they are alive. As long as they are getting along each day, they are fine and whenever death comes knocking, they don't mind going.

I cannot forget one of the days God was teaching me on the **AUTHORITY OF A BELIEVER**, and He said something that shook me greatly then. **"A king who lacks knowledge that he is a king can of course be manipulated by his slave"**. Your knowledge over a matter can grant you mastery in that area.

One of the factors that can render a man worthless is ignorance. No wonder so many have surrendered to the slavery of the enemy because they lack knowledge of their standing in Christ Jesus. Some are sick today because they lack knowledge of their divine health in Christ, while so many are poor also simply because of the lack of knowledge on financial principles that can liberate them from the shackles of poverty.

Scriptures says, we are seated with Christ in heavenly places far above principalities and powers.

Satan has no authority to toss your life about like ping pong. The understanding of any realm, grants you access into that realm. You can never make use of any power or authority you are ignorant of.

When you know that you have authority over the devil, then and only then, can you exercise your authority over him and he would obey. This was why the fellow who was not even among the disciples of Jesus was able to cast out devils in the name of Jesus as recorded in Mark 9 vs 38. It was rather because, he had an understanding of the authority in the name of Jesus. Knowledge brings power.

The bible says *"Wisdom is the principal thing, therefore get wisdom; and with all thy getting get understanding" – Proverbs 4:7*

The devil can keep you comfortable, shining as the moon if you lack the understanding that you are meant to shine as the sun.

"… In all thy getting get understanding…" and I would like to add, in all the understanding you get, get an understanding of thy self.

FOR I KNOW

A life of an undiscovered purpose is an unlived life and an unlived life is invariably a worthless one. You may never get to live your life to the fullest until you get the proper knowledge of who you are.

Remembering one of those growing up experience when I would do a specific thing and my parents would shout and ask "don't you know you are a boy?" Or see a girl doing a particular thing especially like standing up to urinate and she would be asked, "Don't you know you are a girl?"

Why were our parents so keen to inculcate such in us? It was rather for the true knowledge and understanding of who we are to be rooted deep inside us, so that we can live our lives to the fullest: and just like our earthly parents would do, God also wants you to come to an understanding of who you truly are and live it to the fullest.

The question remains "Don't you know?" Jesus always asked the question, "Have you not read?"

> **"HAVE YOU NOT READ what David did,**
> **when he was an hungered, and they that were**
> **with him" – Mathew 12 vs 3 (ERV)**

> **"in reply he said, HAVE YOU NOT READ that**
> **he which made them at the beginning made**
> **them male and female" – Mathew 19:4**

> **"...DID YOU NEVER READ in the scriptures, that**
> **the stone which the builders rejected, is become**
> **the head of the corner?"- Mathew 21:42**

To his disciples he asked "are you also without understanding?" (Math 15 vs 16). Jesus would certainly not ask such questions if He was not an apt student of the scriptures too. Recall at the age of twelve when Joseph and Mary took him for the Passover, scriptures said he was seen speaking with the teachers and asking them questions. *"...they found him in the temple courts, sitting among the teachers, listening to them and asking them questions" – Luke 2:46*

He had questions to ask and answers to give also simply because he had read. Again in Hebrews 10:7, we also see Him responding to what was written about him.

> **Then I said, 'See, I have come to do your**
> **will, O God' In the volume of the scroll this is**
> **written about me. – Hebrews 10:7 (ISV)**

God desires that we come to the knowledge of certain truths about ourselves so we can get to say like our Lord "For I know". *"Jesus answered and said unto them, though I bear record of myself, yet my record is true: for I know..." – John 8:12*

FOR I KNOW – WHO I AM

The question "who are you?" has been one of the greatest and permit to say most unanswered questions of all times.

So funny you will see people who lack the slightest idea of who they are, bragging during conflicts and asking themselves with raised shoulders "do you know me?" how much it makes me laugh when people say such, makes me feel like going closer to ask the person in all humility "please sir/ma, who are you really?" and sure you can imagine the kind of answer to expect from such.

Who you are does not lie in the portfolio you carry. The real YOU is not in the position you are occupying. You are not that job you are doing neither are you what others think of you. We can even see the psalmist had such concerns when he said in psalms number 8:4.

"What is man, that thou art mindful of him? And the son of man, that thou visitest him? –   Psalms 8:4 (KJV)

We also see Jesus asking his disciples "who do men say I am?" and even after their response, he asked them again, and "who do you say I am?"

DON'T LET OTHERS DEFINE YOU

"And Simon peter answered and said, thou art the

Christ, the son of the living God. And Jesus answered and said unto him, blessed art thou Simon Barjona: for flesh and blood hath not revealed it unto thee, but my father in heaven." – Mathew 16:16-18 (KJV)

From that scripture, we get to understand that the views the other disciples had about His person, did not really matter to Jesus, because He already knew who he is.

It cannot be argued, of course he knew He is Christ, the son of the living God. The assignment over his head was not dependent on people's views of him. He rather asked the question for them to have an accurate knowledge of Him and not for Him to know Himself.

So many have allowed the totality of their lives be defined by others view about them. You crawl into a shell, hiding your face in shame just because someone somewhere thinks you aren't beautiful enough, so many have zipped their mouths simply because someone felt his opinions are senseless. Awake again, be YOU and stop letting your life be defined by other peoples view and opinions.

"Then spake Jesus again unto them saying, I am the light of the world, he that followeth me shall not walk in darkness but shall have the light of life. The Pharisees therefore said unto him, Thou bearest record of thyself, thy record is not true. – John 8:13 (KJV)

Jesus answered and said unto them, though I bear record of myself, yet my record is true: for I know whence I came and whither I go; but ye cannot tell whence I come and whither I go" – John 8:14 (KJV)

Jesus was bold to say "I AM THE LIGHT OF THE WORLD", it doesn't matter what others think. Whether the Pharisees believed it or not does not change anything. It does not in any way affect who He is. He could only bear record of himself because He had the right knowledge of who he is.

Men can say anything about who they think you are, the good news is, their definition of you doesn't define you unless you let it to. What defines you is who God says you are and that's all that matters. The true definition of our lives lies with our Maker.

In regards to Jesus, some called him Elias, some said he was John the Baptist, some others called him one thing or the other but all those were never definitions of who He is. Even when he revealed his identity and boldly declared "I am the light of the world", they still doubted him.

I can imagine the Pharisee murmur to say "A mere son of a carpenter, how dare you equal yourself to God?"

Beloved I may not know what people have called you, I may not know what descriptions others have given, maybe – that school dropout, that former prostitute, that good for nothing, an "olodo", a nobody, an Illiterate?

Well they may have called you whatever they wanted, whatever they thought you were and they can still call you whatever they want if only you don't see yourself in the light of who they say you are but rather see yourself in the light of who God says you are.

Let me remind you what God calls you in case you don't know or you may have forgotten. God calls you a holy nation, a royal priesthood, a chosen generation. Bringing to your consciousness that you are not a "nobody", rather you were born into royalty not minding your background, you are not a good for nothing, rather you are a chosen generation not minding your past, chosen by God Himself for His good works not minding your qualifications.

"But ye are a chosen generation, a royal priesthood, an holy nation, a peculiar people; that ye should shew forth the praises of him who hath called you out of darkness into His marvelous light-1 Peter 2:9 (KJV)

This same issue was with Saul when he encountered the Lord. Ananais had been sent by the Lord to go speak to Saul, but let's see the argument Ananias put up with the Lord and what the Lord answered him.

"Then Ananias answered, Lord, I have heard by many of this man, how much evil he hath done to thy saints at Jerusalem" – Acts 9:13

Acts 9:15 - But the Lord said unto him, "Go, thy way; for he is a chosen vessel unto me... (KJV)

Acts 9:15 - But the Lord said, Go without fear: for he is a special vessel for me... (BBE)

People may choose to call you anything even based on your past. Ananias said, "Lord, I have heard by many...", he saw Saul based on what people have discussed about him but be rest assured that God does not see you based on peoples descriptions and discussions no matter how right they may be.

Rather God sees you as a chosen vessel, a special instrument chosen for His good works. So when next people call you anything outside what God says you are, don't mind them, but rather smile at them understanding the fact that they are just ignorant of your true personality. The reality of your personality is not in their eyes but in the word.

THE ASSIGNMENT

The true understanding of who you are, is on the understanding of your life assignment. As we would see in the bible, John was appointed to be a fore runner to the messiah, and the understanding of that enabled the fulfillment of that purpose for one cannot fully run and fulfill a purpose, he has not discovered.

As John was called to be a fore runner to the master, he didn't try to become the savior and save the world instead. Jeremiah was called to be a prophet to the nations and the understanding of that helped him in fulfilling that purpose.

Paul was called to be a minster unto the gentiles, Peter was called to also be a minister to the Jews and Jesus was assigned to die on the cross and reconcile men unto God. Everyone has his own unique assignment and that's why we have said that everyone has a purpose but not everyone have discovered theirs and sadly, some may never discover nor walk in the light of their life purposes

A true understanding of self requires a clear understanding of your place of assignment. John speaking in Mathew 11:3 said **"Are you the Christ or we should expect another?"**

I imagine the pain in John's heart as he said those words, I guess he was invariable asking Jesus, do you even know who you are? If yes, then what are you waiting for?" but Jesus also having a clear understanding of who He is and what his purpose is, knew it was not yet time.

Let me quickly add that you should never let anyone rush you into the fulfillment of any life assignment. The purposes of God must follow God's timing.

Hence have you discovered yourself and have you gotten the right knowledge of your assignment? You didn't just come by chance, God created you and brought you to the place where you are currently for a purpose and you need to understand that purpose for which you were made.

Be it in the power sector, education sector, humanities, and so on. There is a place specially designed for you. It is quite disheartening some believers thinks Christians shouldn't be in politics, but then I say, there is someone whose assignment is there. In every sector, God has placed men there to shine His glory though it is also disheartening that so many of these people may have defiled, abandoned or misused their calling.

THE DISTINGUISHING FACTOR

This is one of the reasons many people, even Christians are frustrated.

The struggle in life only comes outside the purposes of God. When you are where He sent you, He supplies you with all you need to be there. Many believers are struggling to make it outside the divine purposes of God for their lives.

I remember God teaching me this during the NCCF national conference in Jos. It was the second day specifically the 19th of September, 2016. The morning session just ended and Dr. Ferdinand Nweke had just introduced the theme of the programme "Ministry of the Holy Spirit". As I looked around, where people in their great numbers, gathered from all the states of the federation. Then the Spirit impressed a thought in my heart.

These multitude gathered here, are just a fraction of the population of graduates that have been pushed into the labour market by their institutions at the same time with me. These people have been pushed into the nation to occupy positions, sit in places and occupy offices but there comes a question, **"WHAT DIFFERENTIATES YOU FROM THIS CROWD?"**

The Spirit continued and said, "Notice that I didn't bring them all out, in a time as this to leave or disgrace them. It is not a coincidence that this multitude has been pushed out at the same time as you but what sets you apart?

Is it having Jesus and being born again? Many of them are. Is it having the Holy Ghost and operating in diverse gifts of the Spirit? Many of them even operate in heights you haven't reached. What then will distinguish you?

You must know that to every man, there is a set path they must walk in. Every individual has his or her unique path to tread.

> *"...He will teach us what he wants us to do; we will walk in the PATHS HE HAS CHOSEN" – Isaiah 2:3b (GNB)*

And no matter how fast you run in the wrong direction, you can never arrive at the right destination. A Turkish proverb would say "No matter how far you have gone in the wrong direction, turn back".

The spirit further explained that this is the reason why many believers who have been called for a glorious purpose get frustrated in their time.

Many would chase after what Elohim have not kept in stock for them, running after things that are not in their destiny pack.

THE PLACE OF PRIMARY ASSIGNMENT

The Lord says in psalm 32:8 **"I will guide you along the best pathway for your life".**

God knows the best pathway for your life and until you let Him lead you in that path as you faithfully follow, you may never ever arrive at your life destination.

> *"And they went each of them straight forward whither the spirit was to go; they went..." – Ezekiel 1:12 (KJV)*

That's the secret my beloved. **"WHITHER THE SPIRIT WAS TO GO, THEY WENT"** But the question is, have you found out where the Spirit want to go in your life?

That work you are so earnestly seeking, is it where the spirit wants to go? Mathew 4:1 says **"Then was Jesus led up of the spirit into the wilderness".**

Jesus already knew He came to die, but did he head straight to the cross to die and save the world after being baptized? No, rather He went where the spirit intended to go.

There is a place prepared for you to shine forth from. Scriptures speaking in Genesis 26:2-3

Genesis 26:2-3 "And the Lord appeared unto hum and said, "Go not down into Egypt; dwell in the land which I shall tell thee of: sojourn in this land and I will be with thee, and will bless thee, for unto thee and unto thy seed, I will give all these countries"

I feel the Lord saying, I will bless you but only where I sent you. The NYSC (National Youth Service Corps) calls it a place of primary assignment (PPA), you must be cleared from your place of primary assignment to receive your allowance. So dearly beloved, where has the Lord sent you? Stop struggling outside the purpose of God for your life.

Discover yourself, discover your life assignment and as you discover it, also find out where you are called to fulfil it. So many ministries have died down simply because they tried being established where God didn't send them, so many visions have been terminated simply because they tried being established where they felt the money flows, not regarding where God had in mind for them.

FOR I KNOW – WHENCE I CAME:

> *Jesus answered and said unto them, though I bear record of myself, yet my record is true: for I know whence I came...- John 8:14 (KJV)*

Jesus was saying, I just know that what I am saying is true because I know where I came from. I said I am the light of the world and I know it is true because whence I came is actually the source of light.

I had a conversation with someone some time ago, and in the course of our conversation, the person asked me what tribe I am from; I answered the person I am from Abia state and he became surprised and didn't believe me. Said I cannot be Igbo, that I don't speak like them and even if I am Igbo then I am too quiet to be from Abia state, that he knows people who come from there to be a bit violent and always try to play sharp. I laughed but I don't actually need his approval for what I said to be true. I am Igbo cause I know where I came from.

Life is a journey. Some say it starts from B to E. with the B representing Birth and D representing death. Then everyone has the same starting point of B but not the same destination of D as there are actually two paths you get to see once you start the journey of life. You either follow the tiny pathway C which represents Christ or you follow the wide road D. the tiny pathway out cuts D and arrives you at E representing Eternity or Everlasting life.

You may never truly tell where you are and where you are going, if you don't know where you are coming from. Abraham instructing his servant, made him swear never to pick a wife for his son from Canaan, rather he should go to the country where he was born and pick a wife there for his son and I began to query myself, aren't there good and evil women everywhere? Shouldn't he had been more interested in his servant picking a God fearing woman for his son? But then I knew, this was a man that had an understanding of where he came from.

Moses could have been lost in pharaoh's palace, dining and wining with the beautiful maidens of Egypt and lose his divine assignment, but his mother ensured Moses had an understanding of who he is and where he came from to discern that he doesn't belong to the palace and that he has an assignment to fulfill.

Don't be like a tree without roots, of course you know it won't stand for long. Discover your roots, know your origin.

Also in knowing whence you came, it is expedient you know the origin of Gods dealings with you. Know how and where the Lord started with you and that can help you to know where you are and what is expected of you.

God told Abram to leave his father's house and follow Him to where He would show him and Abram obeyed. It came to a point where God had to remind Abram from whence he brought him from.

***"Then the Lord said to him, "I am the Lord,
who led you out of Ur in Babylonia to give you
this land as your own"– Genesis 15:7 (GNB)***

So many times would the Lord tell the Israelites, I am the Lord, who brought you out of Egypt, just for them to know, he didn't bring them thus far to forsake them. Beloved can you remember where the Lord picked you from, and compare it to where you are now.

God have not brought you this far just to leave or abandon you here. He surely has a plan for you.

In the cause of fulfilling purpose, you must know where you came from. You must know from whence you started. Men who cannot tell how and where they started from, has no journey and him that has no journey has no destination.

FOR I KNOW – WHITHER I GO

The knowledge of the destination of every individual always triggers hope in the heart of such individual. God woke Abraham up in the night to show him the uncountable stars on the sky, I believe to create a picture of where He is taking him to. Even though you have no heir now, but this is what I have decided to do with you.

This is the position I am bringing you up to. The same happened to Joseph, so many a times would he see in his dreams of his brothers bowing down to his authority even when he lacked understanding of the vision, but I believe that, it was God also painting a picture of where He was taking him to.

You may not understand it now, but the Lord is taking you somewhere. God told the Israelites, I am taking you to a land flowing with milk and honey, and if we could ask any of the elders then, where is this land? They wouldn't know, but they knew God is taking them to a land flowing with milk and honey.

But in regards to the scripture in the context, Jesus was saying, I know who I am because I am the son of the living God, I know whence I came because I came from heaven, and I know whither I go because once my assignment here is accomplished, am headed back to where I came from.

There is need that we also understand that we are spiritual beings planted in this physical world to fulfill a purpose, and we will return to whence we came to give account of how we executed our assignment.

No wonder brother Paul speaking to the Corinthians said *"If in this life only we have hope in Christ, we are of all men most miserable" – 1 Corinthians 15:19*

Our hope in Christ is not in this life alone. We are headed somewhere, it doesn't all end here, and we know where we are going.

KNOW HIM TO KNOW YOURSELF:

Having clearly understood that, to fulfill purpose on earth and achieve your divine God given life assignment, then there is a need to know. Just like Jesus said, "For I know", you need to know. Having a clear knowledge of who you are, clear knowledge of where you came from and an idea of where you are headed.

The knowledge of God is not what we can ever do without in this assignment. There are dimensions of this knowing or truth that God wants us to have, which will never come to you without the knowledge of God.

The sons of Eli were also called "worthless" because they lacked knowledge of God.

"Now the sons of Eli were worthless men who did not know the Lord" – 1 Sam 2:12 (ISV)

By this, I do not mean a mere head knowledge of who God is. For sure the sons of Eli knew God was but they lacked an experiential knowledge of God is. Man can only truly know himself by knowing his creator.

God alone knows the purpose for which he created you and planted you where you are, and only in Him can you ever discover your worth.

And if we must find it out and fulfill it, then we must come to Him to know of it. This revelation was what Job had when he cried out "Where can we learn to understand?" in Job 28:20.

"Where then is the source of wisdom? Where can we learn to understand? No living creature can see it, not even a bird in flight. Even death and destruction admit they have heard only rumours. God alone knows the way, knows the place where wisdom is found, because he sees the end of the earth, Sees everything

under the sky"   *–Job 28:20-24 (GNB)*

Knowledge of self is a product of revelation from divinity. God alone knows the way, he knows where wisdom can be found. That is the reason Jesus told peter, flesh and blood didn't reveal this to you; when peter got the accurate definition of who Jesus is. Because neither flesh nor blood knows where this knowledge is.

The unveiling of your identity only lies in the discovery of Gods personality. . Paul knew Jesus came and died when he was persecuting the church but when he encountered Jesus personally, the true knowledge of his assignment on earth became clear to Him.

It is a waste of lifetime to live outside the plan of God for you. And He who knows what he has planned out for you, He who has the roadmap to your treasured destiny is saying in Psalm 32:8 **"The Lord says, "I will teach you the way you should go. I will instruct you and advice you"**

And how will the Lord teach you? It is by His Spirit.

"Howbeit, when the spirit of truth comes, He will guide you into all truth" - John 16:13 (KJV)

And again, I feel the Lord saying, do not think that you know it all.

"Don't be stupid like a horse or a mule which must be controlled with a bit or bridle to make it submit" – Psalm 32:9 (GNB)

Don't be stupid to think you know the way, don't be stupid to think that you can get there yourself; you have to know and follow the Lord into what he has planned for you.

It is not time to mind what people are saying about you, or what they have called you, but to discover who God says you are and the purpose for which he made you. Discover God, discover yourself, discover your place of assignment, and know your worth. You are precious in God's eyes and your assignment is important in God's agenda and you cannot just afford to fail in it.

Chapter Three
The Transformation Process

CHAPTER THREE

THE TRANSFORMATION PROCESS

Well I may not be so old, or have lived here on earth for long but for the little years I have lived, I have found out that there is no man who gave his life out to God that ever regretted it.

One of my pastors would say, you cannot pass God in giving; meaning you can never give more than God. You give Him a cup of water and he would give you rivers of living water, there is nothing you ever give God which he doesn't multiply back to you. You give him your life, which is just a few years and He gives you everlasting life.

"God never takes away something from your life without replacing it with something better". - Billy Graham

"The best way to multiply what you have, is to hand it over to the Lord Jesus Christ" – Pastor Enoch .A Adeboye

Also I have come to realize, there is no man, God cannot use for mighty works, no matter how worthless such a man may look. I would even say God prefers such people to show his glory. Scriptures say he chooses the foolish things of this world to confound the wise.

The birth of the savior into the house of a mere carpenter was not a mistake, as the whole world was expecting the savior to be born in the palace, but our God chooses the low things of life to confound the high. Just like a potter, he transforms what people call worthless into a valued vessel for His glory.

THE GATHERING:

"But some Jews were jealous and gathered worthless loafers from the streets…"Acts 17:5 (GNB)

How can a potter produce a great vessel without clay? In as much as I try to picture the Lord as the potter and we as the clay, yet our God gives us the choice of coming to Him.

He calls out for him that will answer, so he can make out of that man what He will.

"O house of Israel, cannot I do with you as this potter? Saith the lord, Behold as the clay is in the potter's hand, so are ye in mine hand, O house of Israel." – Jeremiah 18:6 (KJV)

I remember in my young age, we would normally store up empty wine bottles, of course to us, they are now worthless and they were to be disposed, but then we would store them up, waiting for people that buy it from us for very little money, which we spent on snacks.

As a young child, I thought they picked them, refill them with new wine and sell them but later I got a chance to spend some months in a glass industry and there I found out the truth. These broken bottles, glasses etc. make up a part of the raw materials for the new ones.

Also I have seen these set of people who would go to rubbish searching for any piece of metal, you may mistake them for mad men by their appearance but they are there searching for any piece of metal they can get. Ever wondered what they are doing with such?

Well I had such questions too not till I saw a place where these men weigh out their metals and sell it out. Note that these were worthless metals disposed by others but yet valuable to another. Worthless materials but yet still valuable to their maker.

So is the Lord calling out for men, whom the world has disposed, Men whom the world have despised, Men who have been tagged worthless by the world.

"And after these things he went forth, and saw a publican, named Levi, sitting at the receipt of custom:

*and he said unto him, follow me and he left all,
rose up, and followed him" – Luke 5:27-28 (KJV)*

**"And Jesus said unto Simon, Fear not; from
henceforth thou shalt catch men. And when they
had brought their ships to land, they forsook
all and followed him" – Luke 5:10 (KJV)**

For what the Lord desires to do with your life, He is calling out to you in a time as this that you may also forsake all ad follow Him just like His disciples dropped all and followed Him and he turned their lives to a living wonder.

**"Walking alongside the Sea of Galilee, he saw
two brothers, Simon who is called Peter and
Andrew his brother, casting a net into the
sea, for they were fishermen. And he said to
them, "Come after me, and I will make you
fishers of men." - Mathew 4:18-19 (KJV)**

That you come to Him as a clay ready to be used by the potter.

**"Come as living stones, and let yourselves be used
in building the spiritual temple, where you will
serve as holy priests to offer spiritual sacrifices to
God through Jesus Christ" – 1 Peter 2:5 (GNB)**

Come as living stones, you are still usable. If there will be a making, then there must first be a coming to Him in whose hands it is to make men because He can turn the stone which the builders rejected and make it the chief corner stone.

THE MAKING PROCESS:

> *"But some Jews were jealous and gathered*
> *worthless loafers from the streets AND*
> *FORMED a mob..." – Acts 17:5 (GNB)*

Having finished with the gathering of the resources is the making process. I have tried to express that the gathering for the Lord, is a call which anyone who wills should answer. As each and every one of us has their own choices, and the Lord will not force his way into any man's life.

The bible says, He stands at the door and knock, that anyone who wills would open and he shall come in and dine with the person.

Gathering of clay together is not all there is, in making a beautiful vase that people will admire and bring glory to its maker. You can gather all the clay you want, it will never become a vase on its own, you can gather all the raw gold but it would never become a beautiful golden ring on its own.

If Noah had gathered all the woods he could, that would never automatically turn into a boat. Someone had to do some cutting into specifications, nails had to be hit in to join those pieces of wood together.

And as we go through the many patterns and processes, God may use in His making, I want us to hold firm to God's promise of making us. God is determined to make us into mighty instruments for His glory. This we can see from a scripture I love so well, Isaiah 41:14.

Each time I read through this verse, it gives me a reassurance that no matter what my life looks like now, God is still determined to make me and His words will never fail.

"Fear not, thou worm Jacob, and ye men of Israel; I will help thee, saith the Lord, and thy redeemer, the Holy one of Israel.

Behold I WILL MAKE THEE a new sharp threshing instrument having teeth; thou shalt thresh the mountains, and beat them small, and shalt make the hills as chaff." – Isaiah 41:14-15 (KJV)

Though men may have looked down on you, they may have regarded you as nothing, as a worm just as the bible says, but God is saying, "I will make you".

Honestly this scripture is just unimaginable if not by faith. I just couldn't imagine a worm with a sharp threshing teeth that it can thresh the mountains, makes me want to shout "this God is awesome". And this is what God wants to do with your life. Something as inconsequential as a worm but yet used for mighty works. How much more great things the Lord will do with your life if only submitted to him.

Also be careful to note that the process of making is unique to each material, Gods patterns of making is unique dependent on what He intends to achieve out of each life. Never try to compare your dealings with God to His dealings with others. But we must trust God knowing that He knows the best way for our lives, and He knows the best way to make us into powerful instruments all for His glory. So can you surrender your life today for making, God is determined to make you but would you come and also stay for the making processes.

THE DROSS:

> *"Take away the dross from the silver,
> and there shall come forth a vessel for
> the finer" – Proverbs 25:4 (KJV)*

The dross refers to the impurities in silver which cover up the true view of silver.

> *"Remove the worthless things from silver to
> make it pure, and a worker can make something
> beautiful" – Proverbs 25:4 (ERV)*

Worthless things which have succeeded in hiding the true worth of a treasure. For the Lord to make something out of you beloved, then firstly, He has to deal with the worthless issues in your life. Worthless behaviors, worthless attitudes, worthless company, worthless association, etc., you know them.

It may be anger, it may be lust, it may temperance, whatever it may be which have made you look worthless, these are the issues God wants to deal in your life, that He may make something beautiful out of you.

It is worthy to note, that until the dross is removed, there is no resource or material to work with. I haven't been to a refiners place but I have been opportune to watch a potter mold. Having gathered the clay, he runs his hand over the sand to remove anything that is not wanted before he even starts the molding process.

Until those things are removed, the clay is not fit to be used, and I feel the Lord saying, until these issues are dealt with in your life, then your life is not yet totally fit to be used for the beautiful work I intend to make.

Silver with its impurities is worthless, and as costly as gold can be, yet gold in its impurities is worthless.

And this is what the devil has succeeded in doing to many lives, to cover up the glorious worth and beauty God put in them. The devil simply plays with you in the mud, you tend to enjoy yourself with his tricky games but he is simply busy throwing the mud at you, filling your live with mess to cover up your treasure and beauty.

"Now the works of the flesh are manifest, which are these: adultery, fornication, uncleanness, lasciviousness, idolatry, witchcraft, hatred, variance, emulations, wrath, strife, sedition, heresies, envyings, murders, drunkenness, revellings, and such like: – Galatians 5:19-22 (KJV)

So many who have covered their glorious future with dross just for the pleasure of few minutes of sexual satisfaction, it can be anger, it can be drunkenness, it is all in the name of fun, yet the devil is filling the person's life with so much impurity and making him/her unfit for the master to use.

It can be an addiction, you are struggling with but it is time to say NO to the devil. Those tricky games has got to stop.

"… If anyone makes himself clean from all those evil things, they will used for special purposes because they are dedicated and useful to the master, READY TO BE USED FOR EVERY GOOD DEED" – 2 Timothy 2:21

Being born again is not the end point, coming to Christ is not just all: for your worth to shine forth. Notice the part, I capitalized, it is only when a man has been purged of his dross that he is ready to be used by His Maker.

THE REFINERS FIRE

Having noted that the dross is the worthless waste which covers up the true treasure in a believer, the dealing with this dross to take it out of your life requires a conscious and a subconscious effort.

By this, I mean that you have a part to play even as the Lord plays the end role to make you totally usable for His purpose.

According to the scripture we cited in 2 Tim 2:20, it says "if any man purges himself..." clearly stating that you have a great responsibility to make yourself usable in God's hands.

Also if we look at the book of Malachi 3:3-4, we see God taking responsibility of the removal of the dross in the lives of men.

"And He shall sit as a refiner and purifier of silver, and he shall purify the sons of Levi, and purge them as gold and silver, that they may offer unto the Lord an offering in righteousness. THEN shall the offering of Judah and Jerusalem be pleasing unto the Lord, as in the days of old, and as in former years." – Mal 3:3-4 (KJV)

The need for the removal of this dross and worthless wastes, cannot be over emphasized. As we see in the scripture quoted above, the Levi's is the tribe solely dedicated to performing spiritual rites and the offering of sacrifices to the Lord on behalf of the people. But then, of what use is a sacrifice if it is not accepted? Take note of that word "then".

That's the Lord saying, until I deal with the dross in their lives, their sacrifice is not accepted and beloved we know that if their sacrifice is not accepted, then their assignment is a failure and their life purpose is null and void since they were called and separated for this particular purpose.

Hence I perceive God telling someone through this book, this is no more the time to take this issues lightly, because until the Lord deals with the dross in your life, you are just a light hidden in the bushel. You cannot totally fulfill purpose.

A lady described her experience about that same scripture. She said, having read that scripture, she decided to visit a silver smiths place and see for herself what goes on there to understand better what the bible said by our God sitting as a refiner to refine us.

She explained that the silversmith never takes his eyes off that piece on fire, he keeps his eyes on it and knows the piece is ready only when he sees his image on it.

In other words, God keeps us in his refiners' fire and fixes his eyes on us until His image is formed in our lives.

In the journey of life, talent is never enough to fulfill destiny. No matter how good you may be, God still has to deal with the dross in your life that his image may be fully formed and seen in you and your true beauty revealed.

God will never do for you, what you have to do by yourself and you can never ever do what only God can do. God will not off that television for you when you should be studying, God will not slap that pizza out of your mouth before you recognize you are being addictive to food unless you force Him anyway and I must warn that you may not like His method.

I lost my phone at some point in school and while I narrated my sad story to my friends thinking they would sympathize with me, they went about praising God. I had become so addicted to my phone then. first thing I do when I wake was to check my social media handles, if someone dropped off a message and I would be at it till I get reminded that I haven't had my quiet time.

Though I did not understand it at first but quite later when I recognized the damages my phone has caused me and my spiritual walk with God, I joined my friends to thank God for delivering me from it.

I say this to further iterate the point that, in this walk of putting away every dross, you must have to be intentional about it.

There will be sacrifices you must make even as God brings His words to you in diverse measures just to clean you. There may be friends you may be forced to let go, you may need to put away your phone for some time, it may require you to reject food at some other times, you may have to get up and night even when you are still very sleepy but whatever comes with this task, brace up and be ready for it as God works in and out of you, to bring you pure.

Keep your eyes on the goal, and the goal is to be used for special purposes. You are special, and you were made for a special purpose, your assignment is a special assignment but your dross must be taken away.

CHAPTER FOUR

NO EXCUSE

CHAPTER FOUR

NO EXCUSE

There is absolutely no reason why you should end up in the slums of life. There is absolutely no excuse you have to give why you failed or even why you should fail in life. Let me quickly remind you again, that there is an expectation over your life and you cannot afford to fail God, because He has stocked up so much treasure in you and wants you to show forth his Excellency.

I need you to have an understanding, that you are not a "good for nothing" as others may have branded you, you are not worthless, but rather you were created for a purpose. The world needs you. You are the light of this world, you are the taste the world is seeking for.

Whatever excuse you think you have, there are men who have passed through worse situations and came out strong to make an impact on their world. Has the world knocked you down? Get up and hit again. Excuses are cages, excuses are prisons but funny enough, many individuals have been imprisoned by themselves with excuses and then blame it on the devil.

Even if, there is nothing more I may get to tell you here, remember that there is a promise over your life, and that promise is God saying "I will make you" and God is committed to fulfilling His word.

"Fear not, thou worm Jacob, and ye men of Israel; I will help thee, saith the Lord, and thy redeemer, the Holy one of Israel.

Behold I will make thee a new sharp threshing instrument having teeth; thou shalt thresh the mountains, and beat them small, and shalt make the hills as chaff." – Isaiah 41:14-15 (KJV)

Don't let the devil deceive you beloved with his filthy lies. Has the devil told you lies that you have no one? Remember even Esther was an orphan in a strange land but the Lord picked her up just like a worm and made her the queen of a nation.

Maybe you feel you are hated by everyone, no one loves you and you have looked down at yourself and have shrinked yourself into a world of pity, beloved it is time to say NO to the devil tactics and remember that Joseph was even hated by his own brothers, Jesus was hated even by his own creature, the very ones he came to save.

Maybe you are the least in the house, or peradventure with a disability and you have given up on life, also remember that even Naaman was a man with disability yet he was a general and a commander of men.

Jesus is still in the business of making men. He is ever ready to turn you into a living wonder.

Get rid of those excuses the devil may have filled your minds with and focus on Jesus who can make even the least and down trodden into a living wonder.

I WILL HELP YOU

We cannot make ourselves, no matter how hard we try. No matter who anyone thinks he is or whatever level anyone feels he has attained, someone else played a role to bring that person to such a height or position. God wants us to do away with any excuse because He wants to help us.

Just like the mindset Gideon had, when the angel of the Lord told him of a purpose he had to fulfill, are you also asking Lord how can I?

"Gideon replied, "But Lord, how can I rescue Israel? My clan is the weakest in the tribe of Manasseh, and I am the least important member

of my family. The Lord answered, "YOU CAN DO IT BECAUSE I WILL HELP YOU.

You will crush the Midianites as early as if they were only one man" – Judges 6:15-16 (GNB)

God is saying "I will help you", just as He said "I will make you". For the assignment He has placed over our lives, He is saying you can do it, not because we have the strength and capacity to do it but because He is ever read to walk with us in the course to help us fulfill it such that our whole hope should be trusting in the Lord's promise and his capacity to help us.

Whatever excuse you have, search the scriptures and you will see such people who surrendered to the Lord and the Lord picked them as a worm and made them threshing instruments to mountains.

We also see Moses bringing up his excuse when he was called for his life assignment and the reply was still, "I will help you".

"But Moses said, "No, Lord, don't send me, I have never been a good speaker, and I haven't become one since you began to speak to me, I am a poor speaker, slow and hesitant."- Exodus 4:10

The Lord said to him, "who gives man his mouth? Who makes him deaf or dumb? Who gives him sight or makes him blind? It is I, the Lord. Now go! I WILL HELP YOU to speak and I will tell you what to say" – Exodus 4:11-12 (GNB)

If you study the chapter prior to the one we just cited, in Exodus

3:11, we see Moses telling God, **"I am nobody, how can I go to the king and bring the Israelites out of Egypt?"** Moses was saying "Lord I am so worthless, I am certainly not qualified for this work you are calling me to do, but the Lord replied and told Moses, "I will be with you".

And just like Moses so many of us are also saying, Lord I am worthless. The purpose and the assignment you have placed on my life, cannot be achieved by my kind of person. Lord, this task is so heavy that I don't see how it can ever be fulfilled in my life and the Lords gentle reply has been that the fulfillment of our assignment does not lie in our abilities but in His abilities to help us.

Beloved it is not about you but about what the Lord can do with your life. For whatever weakness you may mention, God is still saying, "I will help you" to fulfill that expectation which I have over you. It is not just by your abilities, for who He calls, He equips him.

God is more than able to bring to pass whatsoever He has said concerning your life. When the Lord was talking to Abraham and told him "I will make you a father to nations" I am so sure Abraham didn't get to understand. How can I be a father to nations when I am not even yet a father to one? But that never stopped the fulfillment of God's word.

I recall Pastor David Oyedepo sharing his testimony, that when God told him about Canaan land, his congregation was not yet even up to a thousand but yet today we see that prophecy fulfilled.

Pastor E.A Adeboye asked the Lord for a place but rather God promised him a city, then it sounded so unimaginable but yet our God is one who speaks and it comes to pass. God can never make a promise He is not ready to keep, He does not say things He doesn't mean.

Hence beloved, God is capable of establishing that which he has spoken concerning you, only if you will agree to walk with him in faith. And guess what he is saying… I love to round it up in four words, "I WILL MAKE YOU".

I so much love personalizing that scripture in Isaiah 41:14-15, *"Fear not, thou worm DAVID, and ye men of Israel; I will help thee, saith the Lord, and thy redeemer, the Holy one of Israel. Behold I will make thee a new sharp threshing instrument having teeth; thou shalt thresh the mountains, and beat them small, and shalt make the hills as chaff."*

Even when it seems, all is not working out the way I want, I gain strength knowing that the Lord has promised to make me and He is able and more than able to bring his word to fulfillment in my life. I trust in his capacity to bring to pass that which He has spoken over my life.

God can never and I repeat, can never fail in His words. Has he said it? Then you can be so sure that He will do it. And He has certainly said that He will make you, He has also said that He will help you. Hence kick out that fear, and let's hold God by his word which can never fail.

CHAPTER FIVE

DISCIPLESHIP – GOD'S TOOL IN MAKING MEN

CHAPTER FIVE

DISCIPLESHIP – GOD'S TOOL IN MAKING MEN

Searching through the scriptures, I came to discover that most of the men who God ever transformed from worthlessness to mighty men were men who submitted to discipleship. No man can ever make himself. And one of the tools which I have discovered God uses in His making of men is DISCIPLESHIP.

Discipleship is simply the believing and following of a leader. The two major words here are "Believing" and "Following". There is certainly no need following someone you don't believe in.

If you are going to follow me to a particular destination, it means you are following me believing that we will arrive at our destination such that even if I don't know the way, you believe in my abilities to find the way and go the way.

You wouldn't follow me if you were sure, I can never arrive at the right destination. These two factors must work in tandem with each other. If you believe without following, your life will not be properly disciple and in the same vein, if you follow without first believing, your life will not also be correctly disciple.

Even the scriptures say *"...him that cometh to the father must believe that He is and He is a rewarder of those who diligently seek Him" – Hebrews 11:6.* All through the scriptures, we would see men and women who believed and followed a leader so that they too could see the path of greatness and walk therein.

DAVID AND HIS MEN

"And everyone that was in distress and every one that was in debt, and everyone that was discontented, gathered themselves unto him, and he became a captain over them: and there were with him about four hundred men" - 1 Samuel 22:2 (KJV)

The message bible called them misfits of all kind. Looking at the description of these men that gathered themselves about David, we get to see that these were men that were dejected and rejected. *"Not only that, but all who were down on their luck came around – losers and vagrants and misfits of all sorts. David became their leader. There were about four hundred in all – 1 Samuel 2:22 (MSG)*

Probably the society has termed them worthless and useless. Men who were dissatisfied, men who have tried their best in so many things but yet failed in so many things and so many times and they have looked at themselves as losers. Misfits of all sorts.

It may have been ladies who have been sexually abused all their lives, it may be our young boys and girls addicted to drugs, they were not good for anything, worthlessness was written all over them but these men picked up themselves and submitted themselves to David.

They believed David and followed him. The bible says David became a captain over them.

These men who were misfits became fit for mighty works, these men who had failed in so many things and so many times became victorious and conquerors.

> ## *"These are the names of David's mighty warriors..." – 2 Sam 23:8*

Mighty things were said of these men in the later end of their lives according to 2 Samuel 23:8-29. Some time ago, they were misfits, just a few years from then, the bible called them mighty warriors, WHY? Simply because they believed and submitted to a leader.

JEPHTHAR AND HIS MEN

Jephthar and his men are another example of the kind of transformation that can take place in a man's life when he submits to right leadership.

"Jephthar fled from his brothers and lived in the land of Tob. There he attracted a group of worthless men, and they went round with him" – Judges 11:3 (GNB)

You may wonder, why these men were called worthless, yet their acts were mighty. Jephthar being the son of a prostitute, his brothers of course saw nothing good in him. To them, he was as worthless as anything and they wouldn't let him inherit anything, but Jephthar never looked down on himself. Others may have looked down on him, but he wouldn't look down on himself.

He fled and gathered men, who probably had also fled from their various houses.

He strayed into the streets to gather men of his kind. Rejected but not dejected men, though crushed but not destroyed, and they turned the whole city around.

Hence beloved, in whose company are you? Who exactly have you believed and who are you following? there is someone out there who can see beyond your uselessness to bring forth something mighty out of you, there is someone out there, who can see beyond your incapability to harness your capabilities, beyond you not being qualified, but can tap into the wealth of your inner self to bring forth that shining pearl everyone who will be marveled to behold in you.

Always remember that who you follow, to some extents determines what follows you.

"Whosoever keeps company with the wise, become wise but a companion of fools suffers harm" – Proverbs 13:20 (ISV)

Walk with the wise and become wise, keep company of great thinkers and become one, in the same vein, keep company with fools as well and become one.

Thus it agrees with the saying, *"show me your friend, and I will tell you who you are"* because one tends to become whatever company one keeps, whether wise or foolish.

ELIJAH AND ELISHA

Elisha could have been a shepherd all his life with no generational impact until Elijah came his way and he willingly followed. A loving attribute about the followership of Elisha is that at the point of his calling, he went back to clear his animals which is an indicator that no matter what happens, there is no going back.

"So Elisha turned back, took the pair of oxen, sacrificed them, boiled their flesh using the farm implements for fuel, and gave the food to the people with him. Then he got up, followed Elijah, and became his servant" – 1 Kings-19:21 (ISV)

An indicator that even if my expectations of this followership is not met, there is absolutely nothing for him to fall back to. Bob Sorge highlighted in his book, the secret of the secret place, that one of the greatest secrets to intimacy with God in the secret place, is the secret of NO PLAN B.

We must come to a point where we follow wholeheartedly without an alternative plan. This we will also discuss in the remaining part of this chapter.

No wonder when Elijah was about to be taken, even though the other sons of the prophets knew that he was about to be taken, but they didn't care much, maybe because to them, even if our leader goes, we can return to what we used to do.

But to Elisha, he knew that there was nothing else left for him to return to, there was NO PLAN B, he would have made a fool of himself to leave all to follow and at the end there was nothing to show and hence Elijah MUST not leave him empty.

"A group of prophets who lived there went to Elisha and asked him, "Do you know that the LORD is going to take your master away from you today?" "Yes, I know," Elisha answered. "But let's not talk about it." – 2 Kings 2:3 (GNB)

This is the course he had chosen and he was determined to make the best out of it. And at the end of the followership, we saw God's promise of making a man fulfilled in his life as those who we could regard as his classmates in the school of prophets came and bowed down to him.

The fifty prophets from Jericho saw him and said "The power of Elijah is on Elisha!" they went to meet him, bowed down before him – 2 kings 2:15 (GNB)

True followership unleashes power, there is no limit to what God can do with a man who submits to be trained. The examples we can mention are too numerous.

This long aged or rather ageless tool and God's strategy is also seen in the scripture, that even in the New Testament, we also see this strategy at play as God turned all those who surrendered from worms who have no ability to mighty threshing tools for His Glory.

In as much as God desires to use the medium of discipleship in making men, yet so many who do not understand these things have toyed with this strategy and ended up marring their lives.

Such men as Gehazi who followed Elisha but would not let the rudiments and principles of discipleship be properly rooted in him. Gehazi was one whose names could also have been written in the sands of time just like Elijah and Elisha who treaded the path before him but he wouldn't sit to learn. His mind wandered away from the lessons to the benefits and ended up learning the lessons the hard way.

THE JEWS AND THE RUFFIANS

"But some Jews were jealous and gathered worthless loafers from the streets and formed a mob. They set the whole city in uproar..." – Acts 17:5 (GNB)

The men as we read about in Acts 17:5 lacked value provided the society was concerned, they were of no use but the jealousy in the hearts of the Jews discovered their worth which no other man could see.

They found out their value, and harnessed it to fulfill their evil desires, that their acts were heard of throughout the city. These men were wild, they didn't carry out any righteous act but yet their names have been engraved in the scriptures.

Permit me to say because they submitted to take instructions from an instituted authority.

That scripture so much convinces me that just as the Lord is scouting for men rejected and dejected by the world whom He can use for His mighty works, so is the devil also seeking for such men that he may also use them for his dubious acts.

There is so much value in those men whom the world may have tagged "worthless". You see that smoker, smoking out his life in one dark corner is a precious asset to the devil as long he keeps him from seeing the glorious light of God's word.

The devil understands the damage that one man can cause his kingdom if he repents and he understands also what a damage he can use such a soul to cause the kingdom of our God.

This explains the reason why former cultists who received Christ joins the Thunder Bolters in school and they can stake out their lives for it to see that others come out from such hooks and deceit of the enemy.

Little wonder, people from other religions or former Muslims go all out notwithstanding the risk when they encounter Jesus.

They are virtually very radical for the kingdom. It is also such men the devil is scouting for because he also knows that when he needs a suicide bomber to massively take lives in one church, such men can go, taking their own lives just to obey their master and fulfill their task.

JESUS AND HIS DISCIPLES

Wrapping it up with our savior Jesus and his disciples, considering the caliber of people Jesus chose in his ministry. Amongst them were fishermen, tax collectors and so on.

"Walking alongside the Sea of Galilee, he saw two brothers, Simon who is called Peter and Andrew his brother, casting a net into the sea, for they were fishermen. And he said to them, "Come after me, and I will make you fishers of men." - Mathew 4 vs 18-19 (KJV)

These men walked with Jesus, even when the Lord was saying, 'the Son of Man has no place to lay His head" they still didn't turn their backs. They submitted to the master and did God fail in his promise of making them fishers of men? Absolutely NO.

They became worms transformed into mighty threshing instruments. Jesus turned their lives to a living wonder that when men saw them again, they marveled. Hallelujah

Beloved, can the reason why you are still where you are, simply be because you have refused to submit yourself to be discipled? No one is overseeing the affairs of your life and hence you have been left the way you are.

No man ever crowns himself king. No matter how mighty a prince is, no matter how qualified he may be, no matter how huge and strong he thinks he is, he must still bend his head for the king makers in order to be crowned king.

The king makers may not be kings themselves, teaching us that, you may be richer, you may be prettier, you may be mightier, or even older than your king makers, but if you must be crowned king my dear, you must bow your head to them.

The making of Moses had to take place in Jethro's house, if not Moses wasn't yet ready. Paul became born again, and it was necessary he went to the apostles even before he started ministry. Discipleship has always been one of God's pattern of making men.

Never think that you already know too much to be trained, never think you are too anointed to be discipled. Never think you are too old to submit to another.

Even Jesus Himself was not left out, scriptures says he learned what it was like to be under God's orders.

"Though he were a Son, yet learned obedience by the things which he suffered. – Hebrews 5 vs 8 (KJV)

And though he was a Son, through the pain which he underwent, the knowledge came to him of what it

was to be under Gods orders. Hebrews 5 vs 8 (BBE)

Jesus too submitted Himself to learn of the Lord.

NO PLAN B

One of the reasons why people don't succeed in discipleship is the assurance of backup plan.

At the back of their minds, they are already saying "if this don't work, then I am going back". If the going gets tougher than I thought, then I am going back, if this gets too burdensome, then I am going. Such people don't ever last in the school of discipleship.

God never promised us of the course of discipleship to be easy, smooth and without inconveniences. Even Jesus Himself followed through with many sufferings. We must come to God as our only source of hope and strength. That we consciously bring ourselves to the point of no return, no matter the pain.

Can you imagine the three Hebrew boys in Babylon saying to the King, "Oh king, we would not bow to your golden image, our God will deliver us" and then at the back of their minds, they are saying, "Oh Lord, we are going to trust you to deliver us but let's also find an escape route peradventure you don't arrive here on time."

Sacrificing his livestock and livelihood was Elisha's way to ensure, he endures to the end. He made away with every backup, paving way for just one course and focusing on it. Peter and the other disciples almost lost focus when Jesus died and peter said to the other disciples, "I am going a fishing" in John 21:3.

Simon Peter said to the others, "I am going fishing." "We will come with you," they told him. So they went out in a boat, but all that night they did not catch a thing – John 21 vs 3 (GNB)

You can imagine that after saying "Ah! Lord, we have left all to follow you" and in this following, even if it will cost us our lives Lord we are ready to die with you in Mathew 19:27 and Mark 14:31.

Then Peter answered and said to Him; Behold we have forsaken all, and followed thee; what shall we have therefore? – Math 19:27 (KJV)

Peter answered even more strongly, "I will never say that, even if I have to die with you!" And all the other disciples said the same thing.   – Mark 14:31 (GNB)

You can see the tone in Peter's language as he asked "… what shall we have therefore?" that when Jesus was crucified and buried, I can imagine the thoughts going on in his heart asking again "Is this what we are to have?" since it was our boats and nets that we left to follow, they are still there at the riverside, we can as well return to our fishing.

I also marveled at what exactly was going on in Elisha's mind as he followed his master Elijah while he divided the seas for them to walk through, knowing so well that if his master is taken without releasing his power, he may be stuck at the other side and probably die off there, but in it, I see a man whose heart was made up, a man in whose heart is saying, 'if this is the end, then so be it.

I have no life outside this course. There is nothing else to fall back to."

The same life we would see as it regards to Ruth and Naomi. That when Ophrah kissed her mother-in-law goodbye to return to her people, Ruth held on. And even when Naomi was asking her to leave saying your sister have returned to all that she left before embarking on this journey, Ruth please follow her.

*... Look, your sister-in-law has returned
to her people and to her gods, follow your
sister-in-law – Ruth 1 vs 15 (RV)*

*But Ruth answered, "Stop urging me to abandon
you and to turn back from following you.
Because wherever you go, I'll go. Wherever you
live, I'll live. Your people will be my people,
and your God, my God: – Ruth 1:16 (KJV)*

But the cries of Ruth was heard in response to that. A cry that "if this is where I meet my end, then so be it". A cry of "Dear mother-in-law, I have nothing to fall back to. Before I engaged in this journey, I had no PLAN B. I have held my hands on the plough and there is no looking back."

God desires to see our singularity of purpose in regards to following him. Can we re-examine our following and ask ourselves if we sincerely left all to follow. What have we set up in our hearts as a backup plan? What's the plan B that we have secretly kept aside in case of eventualities in our journey?

It may be the money in your account, it may be a promise from someone, it can be that health insurance, your friends, etc. I also think it was for this reason that Jesus told his disciples not to carry any purse when He sent them out in two's in Luke 9:3. He was specific enough to say, "Carry nothing for the trip" and in this journey too, God is saying once more "CARRY NOTHING".

*He told them, "Don't take anything along on
your trip—no walking stick, traveling bag, bread,
money, or even an extra shirt. – Luke 9:3 (ISV)*

So many a times, we seek to help God fulfill His promises to us that we end up going into error. Abraham went into error, when the thought of a plan B arose.

Since God have promised him to be father of many nations, let him at least be a father of one boy through the Plan B and maybe before he dies, he may have become father to many nations as was promised him.

Today, God is saying, you don't need an alternative plan. Even as He has promised to make you and this making requires your following, yet you must follow with a singularity of purpose.

CHAPTER SIX

THE QUARRY

CHAPTER SIX

THE QUARRY

The quarry is a place where stones for construction are shaped and prepared. One thing that happens in the quarry is that each stone is made to perfectly fit in so that you don't have to hit any stone to enter where it should.

"The stones with which the temple was built had been prepared at the quarry, so that there was no noise made by hammer, axes or any other iron tools as the temple was being built" – 1 kings 6:7 (GNB)

The bible says this was done so that there would be no noise in the temple. Hence this scripture also explains why there is so much noise in the world today?

So disheartening we now have ministers making no impart but making noise on the altar of our God.

So sad we now have worshippers whose worship doesn't even break through the roof, talk more of ascending to the heavens.

Noise makers even in the place of prayer, prayer warriors whom with all the tongues yet cannot communicate to the father. Noise makers in the Temple. Noise makers at the senate, noise makers in many sectors of the world.

No wonder there is so much noise in the world today. Lesbians have gotten a say in our world of today, homosexuals now have a right in our society today, and I begin to wonder, where were the Christians in politics when these laws were being made? That we now have ministers of the gospel being persecuted for upholding God's laws by not joining such people and it pains my heart.

Just as we have mentioned in the chapters above, that there is a place of assignment for every individual, there is a place you are designed to fit in but it is quite unfortunate that most people are only making noises in their different areas of assignment because they did not allow themselves to be properly trimmed to successfully fit into their divine calling.

Pastor Nathaniel Bassey made a post on Facebook, as he admonished music ministers. Earlier in his ministry as a music minister, he had an offer to go minister abroad, but his pastor then quickly refused it noting that he was not ready yet.

He quite felt bad then but had to obey the instructions of his pastor, and now he appreciates his pastor for not letting him go then as he would have been an utter disgrace now. And I quickly thought, maybe the pastor Nathaniel Bassey would have just been another noisy music minister but thank God he endured his quarry and came forth a finished work for our generation and the world in general.

I write this to let you know, that when you discover that God-given assignment for your life, it is designed that you fit in properly and make the needed impact that there shall be no noise, but for this purpose to be actualized, you cannot afford to escape the quarry.

The quarry is as well a place of making, it is a place of trimming, cutting down of excesses. I call it the Lord's divine institute of training. There are certain excesses you cannot afford to carry, if you must fulfill purpose. Let us see a few examples of men who faced their quarry.

JOSEPH

I see Joseph as a man who God started preparing from his father's house to take over the economy of Egypt. The plan of God for Joseph's life was clearly seen, which was to bring him to a high place where he can be used to save the economy of nations, which God even showed Joseph through his dreams.

Little wonder, he had the dream of the sheaves which pertains to agriculture and then the dream of the stars and moon which pertains to position but Joseph never understood.

"...I had another dream. In which I saw the sun and the moon and eleven stars were bowing down to me" – Genesis 37:9 (GNB)

But have you ever pondered on why did God had to take him to that throne through the prison. What was the purposes for all the sufferings he suffered in Egypt?

The answer is not far from the fact that God was preparing Joseph in His quarry. Right from Potiphar's house, God began to deal with him on how to handle and control men as he became the personal attendant to Potiphar in Egypt (Gen 39 :4), on how to face pressures and as well cope with emotional imbalance coming from Potiphar's wife.

> *"So day after day she spoke with Joseph,*
> *but he never consented to lie with her or*
> *to remain with her" – Genesis 39:10*

Day after day, Joseph faced these harsh conditions, he needed to gain his stand amidst the pressures and the emotional imbalance because God knew that one day, Joseph will be needed to make a critical decision amidst an emotional imbalance coming from his family and his people.

As Joseph suffered these things, it did not in any way show that God was not with him, as people would usually assume that when things are not working out pleasantly for someone, then God has turned His back on such an individual rather Gen 39:21 says *"but the Lord continued with Joseph..."* which shows us that it was God carefully taking Joseph through the process.

Systematically dealing with his life in the areas of people management, pressure control, anger control, emotional balance and everything he may have needed to learn in order to successfully fulfil the assignment he was destined for.

No wonder at the end, he could declare to his brothers that all these while, it was God's master plan being played out.

> *"But as for you, ye thought evil against me;*
> *but God meant it unto good, to bring to*
> *pass, as it is this day, to save much people*
> *alive"*   *– Genesis 50:20 (KJV)*

MOSES

Just like Moses too, certain experiences we pass through ends up preparing us for the task ahead. The many occurrences in Moses's life played their roles in thoroughly equipping and preparing him for the journey ahead.

I am so sure, God was certain about his strategy in dealing with the Egyptians, and for every plot He had in mind, He needed to prepare a man to accomplish it. God allowed Moses to grow in the palace, granting him access and understanding about the nature of the people He would still come back to face. One that would not take to His heels when the Egyptian magicians turn their staff to snakes.

Being a palace boy, he had seen it all, he may have even known those magicians by their names, such that when God revealed Himself, he was sure he had seen a mightier one.

Moses faced cruelty, he saw wickedness and though he had a meek heart but yet, God needed one who wouldn't be meek on His enemies.

One who wouldn't be shaking to hit the red sea such that it swallows up his enemies in battle and by the time Moses had killed an Egyptian and was on the run for his life, I see God bringing a man to have the feel of fear that his people were passing through.

> *"Then Pharaoh heard about it, and he attempted to kill Moses; but Moses ran away from Pharaoh and went to dwell in the land of Midian, and he sat down by a well" – Exodus 2:15*

If I was going to raise a man in whom I can trust not to fear the face of pharaoh, then he must understand what it means to fear and be afraid of him. At a time, Moses was running from Pharaoh and the next, Moses was facing pharaoh without fear.

Running to a faraway land, Moses became a shepherd. Having experienced fear, God started taking him through the leadership course and even the advanced leadership course using Jethro's flock.

The skills needed to tend for people in wilderness, he learnt even as he tended the flock during that course so that by the time God guilds His people to their promised land like a flock, He can entrust them into Moses hands whom He had groomed.

> *"You were guiding your people like a flock, by the hand of Moses and Aaron" – Psalm 77:20*

Though Moses was a man meek at heart but God as well knows that talents and attributes/temperaments can never take the place of skill and experience. The place of preparation is such that the purposes of God can fully find expression even though unfortunately, Moses failed in his anger management course.

DAVID

The life of David also shows us the magnitude of what God can do with a life, He has prepared in His quarry.

In the secret of the bushes, God trained David as he tended his father's flock. At times God will bring the bears and lions along his path so that by practice, David may master the skill of the sling.

And in the course of David mastering the sling, God also showed him the weakness of his sling without His power. God was preparing Him because he knew of the goliath that will arise against his people. Little wonder when he met goliath he said;

> *"… thou comest to me with a sword, and with a*

spear and with a shield; but I come to thee in the name of the Lord of hosts, the God of the armies of Israel, whom thou hast defiled" – 1 Sam 17:1

David had learnt the weakness of his sling in times of training and how to depend on God, no matter He didn't say "I come to you with my sling", that would have been foolishness. God had taught him total dependence on His person but yet do you also notice that God as well needed his mastery in the sling.

His ability to care and tend for the flock would reflect in his care and ability to tend the people God would entrust to his hands.

His understanding and dependence of God both in facing wild animals and Goliath would reflect in his dependence on God when opposition arises as a king.

During his fleeing period, where he gathered men, imparted administrative capacities. His courses there included emotional management, team leadership etc. As he led his group, God groomed him in how he would also lead Israel.

THROUGH THE TOUGH TIMES

Even in our contemporary world today, God have not closed down His school of training. If we can be opportune to hear of God's dealings with our fathers in the faith just as we read of Joseph and the rest in the Bible, then you would see clearly how God prepared them for the different platforms they are currently occupying.

God is still raising men, and as He raises them, he stays with them to thoroughly equip them and train them for the task and goes with them in fulfilling the assignment.

"Whenever the Lord did raised them up judges, THEN THE LORD WAS WITH THE JUDGES, and

*saved them out of the hand of their enemies,
all the days of the judge…" – Judges 2:18*

But today, our world is filled with people who don't desire to be trained but want to shine, people who won't sit to learn, they jump classes in the God's divine institute of training but they want to graduate and be used for mighty works.

Hence dearly beloved, those tough times you are crying about, may be God, preparing you for the journey ahead.

The loving part of the school of the Spirit, which distinguishes it from other institutions of the world is that you never willingly enroll into it and at times you may not even know your course outlines.

You have no idea of the test dates, exam dates nor the graduation dates. God keeps taking you in the journey, carefully and meticulously passing you through all the needed processes, passing you through all the heat and fire, so that at the end He can trust that His will over the assignment on your life will be fulfilled.

Are you passing through a phase where you are crying of pressures all around, may be God taking you on His management or endurance course.

Do you have annoying friends all around you? It may be that God have enrolled you for anger management. Are you facing lack? Never mind, in it, you may learn how to manage even little.

God is not wicked not to equip us with the needed tools for a successful assignment. If endurance is needed in your journey, God must work it out.

If temperance is needed, He will work it out in you, if He needs to pass you through many fires that he may humble and bend you, He won't pity you into not passing you through that fire but He is never going to force it on you.

For every position and situation God brings us, our cry should be, Lord what will you have us to learn in this situation? Help me understand what you intend to teach me so that I won't miss it. See what James had to say in James 1:2 about trouble and life's challenges.

"My friends, be glad, even if you have a lot of trouble. You know that you learn to endure by having your faith tested. But you must learn to endure everything, so that you will be completely mature and not lacking in anything" – James 1:2-4 (CEV)

From the scripture above, I get to notice that people murmur during their tough times and troubles because they lack the knowing that the tough times also has its own purpose which according to James is to teach us endurance and in the fourth verse, it says that we should try to endure everything so we can be COMPLETELY MATURE.

If you have thought of throwing in the towel, please endure a little more so that you don't come out lacking. I love the verse 4 from message bible.

"So don't try to get out of anything prematurely. Let it do its work so you become mature and well developed, not deficient in any way" – James 1:4 (MSG)

No matter the heat of the fire, please don't jump out prematurely.

It may be painful but God wants you to hang on. Remember how He sits on us like the refiner's fire until His image is formed.

If he pities us from the fire, we may never shine and His image won't be formed in us. If He is too merciful and loving not to trim us with those sharp cutting edges, we would not look beautiful. The scriptures says, His word is sharper than any two edged sword piercing even to the joints and marrows and is a discerner of thoughts and intents of the heart.

"For the word of God is living and active, sharper than any double-edged sword, piercing until it divides soul and spirit, joints and marrow, as it judges the thoughts and purposes of the heart" – Hebrew 4:12

I know two edged swords are for battle but good enough, this one is not for the enemy rather it is for us.

He will never be too merciful not to pierce us with His word, no matter how it hurts. That sounds scary right, but at times He has to. It can be likened to our mums tending to our wounds with hot water.

As a boy, I once came back home with a cut after playing football. It was really hurting and my mum could see that I was in pains but no matter how tender my mothers' heart is and how loving her heart goes out to me not to see me in pains, she still knew she had to tend to the wound.

She boiled water and ensured it was the right temperature to be applied on my wound. She would usually dip a towel into the hot water and press into the wound, and no matter how I shouted from the pains and how much she feels for me, yet she knows this is what she has to do. If she is too merciful not to tend to my wounds, then it would deteriorate and become worse.

In the same manner, God in all His loving-kindness has to tend to our souls such that even though we cry, and get tempted to ask Him why?, He still lovingly looks at us and with a smile saying "This is certainly for your good." Even though we fall and get wounded, He still smiles at us saying "though the righteous may fall seven times... GET UP, WE ARE NOT DONE YET"

Night is as important as the day; the sun must be followed by clouds and rains. Nonstop sunshine only creates a desert. We don't enjoy storms, but they're an essential part of a complete life. – BOB SORGE (Secrets of the secret place)

I love singing this song which says I can make it, no matter what I face. And if you are feeling down casted this moment, why don't we sing together. Believe it, it is surely going to help.

You don't have to worry
And don't you be afraid
Joy comes in the morning
Mourning may not last for long
For there is a friend named Jesus
Who will wipe your tears away
And if your heart is broken
Just lift your hands and say

I know that I can make it
I know that I can stand
No matter what may come my way
My life is in your hand.
With Jesus, I can take it
With Him, I know I can stand
No matter what may come my way
My life is in your hand.

CHOOSE YOUR OWN PATH

"Tough times never last but tough people do" is a very popular quote by Robert Schuller but let us try put a balance to it by saying "… but tough people are made by tough times".

A young lady ran to her father in despair, and was crying of how she is fed up with virtually everything. She cried how everything is crumbling to her feet, questioned if God still has the whole world in His hands and if he truly does, why is she passing through all those tough times?.

The father didn't say a word in response to her questions, rather he asked her to go get him some carrots, eggs and coffee.

Handing over the materials to the old man, he proceeded right to the kitchen and beckoned on her to follow. He poured out a little water into three pots and placed them on the stove to heat.

Meanwhile he cut up some carrots and put them into the first pot to boil, into the second pot he put two eggs and then poured some ground coffee into the third pot.

After some minutes, he strained the carrots into a plate, peeled the eggs and poured some strained coffee into a cup. While the young lady was confused why her dad would be making himself a meal when she just complained of all the pains she is passing through, the old man gently said to her. "These three items can teach you something about the way we handle adversity.

The carrots went in strong but got mushy in the boiling water, the egg went in fragile but turned hard in the boiling water too while the coffee changed the water into something desirable. *Which of these are you?* You can decide to shrink and cry, you may choose to let it harden you and harden your heart, or you can also choose to turn your down moments into something desirable.

Everyone passes through tough times but not everyone will come out the same. Some get deranged in their challenges, some get hardened to face their tough times but only a few turn their tough times into something desirable and I would rather have you be among the few who changes their adversity to something desirable.

Franklin Roosevelt though paralyzed from his waist down by polio even before running for office of presidency in the United States still became a four-time president of the United States.

Oprah Winfrey though born into a poor home and sexually assaulted at a young age, raped at the age of nine and got pregnant at the age of fourteen still grew into being ranked the richest African-American of the 20th century. Joyce Meyer faced her challenges but today her stories inspires the world.

Hence, don't let your challenges change you, rather transform your challenges.

FAITH SYSTEM

But here you must also understand, that whatever happens to you in the face of your challenges depends on what you are made up of.

The carrots though hard turned mushy in boiling water because of its make-up, the egg though fragile became hard because of what it is made up of, and the coffee seeds rather changed the boiling into a desirable drink also because of what it is made up of.

What stuff are you made up of? That you saw someone laughing in the face of the same tough times you are crying about, is not because the person does not feel the same pains you are feeling, but the effect of that situation on you is not same as its effect on the other person simply because of the difference in your internal dispositions.

Once again I ask, what stuff are you made of? Your composition is based on the things you have allowed into your life.

What you believe will show in the way you talk, the way you behave and in the way you react to issues. When the storm arose against the boat transporting Jesus and His disciples, the disciples became jittery and in the same situation, Jesus was sleeping.

You may say oh! It is because He is the savior, but then what about

Jonah, that when the other sailors were busy throwing in their belongings into the sea, Jonah was sleeping (Jonah 1:5).

There is a consciousness you will have that can wave away every pressure around you. And that is why I will say, Build your faith system.

Your faith system is what responds to your surrounding challenges. There are two basic areas I would love you to be so careful about in regards to what you allow into your life and they are what you hear and what you see.

The ears and the eyes are two major entrances into the heart of any man. When these two doors are not well guarded, then even unhealthy matters will penetrate into the heart of such a man. And when the inner man structure is collapsed, he cannot stand against the pressures surrounding him.

MIND WHAT YOU HEAR

Everyone usually strives to take care of all the systems in their body, they would drink enough water in care of their digestive system, they would eat fruits to care for their circulatory system and all that but quite a few try to care for their faith system.

For faith cometh by hearing, fear cometh by hearing too. Faith comes by hearing Gods word while fear comes by hearing men's word.

"Faith cometh by hearing and hearing by the word of the Lord" – Romans 10:17

You must build your life upon God's word but not the words of man.

God's word can toughen you in the face of tough situations and then help you change it to something desirable.

His words can comfort you even when it seems all is failing and gives you strength and peace to keep pushing. This is one clear difference between believers and non-believers. Jesus calls it the peace that passeth all understanding that even when a thousand is falling all beside you, you aren't moved because you have heard Him say that *a thousand may fall your right hand and ten thousand by your left but none shall come nigh thee.- Psalms 91:7*

Even when it seems there is nothing left to hope on, and everywhere seems dry of provision, there is a strength from within which reminds you His words which says *"He will supply all our needs according to His riches in glory through Christ Jesus"- Phil 2:19.*

When it seems you have been abandoned and dejected, yet we know that we are not alone. We find strength in His word which says *"I will be with you till the end of days".*

This marvels unbelievers, it is beyond what motivational speakers tell you about attitude. That when they believe we should be giving up, we are still smiling because we have also heard David say "The joy of the Lord is my strength".

For every situation, there is a word from God for it. But we must be careful and attentive to hear Him. He can settle every issue in our hearts, if we can clearly hear what He is saying.

You will only be pulling down you internal defense if all you hear is man's negative words. If all your ears are tuned to the world news and reports of men, then you may not boldly face the world. The world tries to instill fear into you, they tell you of the crumbling economies, they tell of the new deadly diseases, and carry news of wars among nations.

The world tell us the facts but God's words tell us the truth. Tom brown in his book "how to receive from God" gave an acronym for *FACT* as for *False Appearance Contradicting Truth*. Facts will change but truth never changes.

The doctor's diagnosis will change with time. Today it may read positive and tomorrow it turns negative but Gods word remains sure. Today, tomorrow and forever, it will still say "You are healed by His stripes". That bank account statement can change, it may be at the zero today and tomorrow, it is announcing you as one of the richest, but Gods word will never change when it says "He has given us all that pertains to life and godliness".

Remember that what your life is composed of will to some extent determine how you react to life challenges.

SEE DIFFERENTLY

In regards to building your faith system, what you see truly matters. Scriptures said if your vision is clear then your whole body will be full of light.

> *The eye is the lamp of the body. So if your eye is healthy, your whole body will be full of light– Mathew 6:22 (ISV)*

When peter heard the Lord, in the midst of the storm, his response to it changed.

> *By this time the boat was in the middle of the sea and was being battered by the waves, because the wind was against them – Mathew 14:24 (ISV)*

> *Jesus said, "Come on!" So Peter got down out of the boat, started walking on the water, and came to Jesus – Mathew 10:29 (ISV)*

Peter started off well in response to the storm after hearing Jesus speak to him that instead of jittering, he rather walked on the sea.

> *But when he saw the wind boisterous, he was afraid; and beginning to sink, he cried, saying, Lord, save me. – Mathew 10:30 (KJV)*

But by reason of what he saw, he began to sink. What peter heard could change his response to the storm but it could not keep him floating.

This is why I wouldn't stop at tell you to hear God speak over your situation, but even as you have heard Him, it is as well expedient that you mind what you see.

Imagine a strong wind coming against two fellows. One fellow sees the wind and get gripped by fear as he has seen a force that is going to blow him away while the other sees the same strong wind and smiles because he has also seen a great force that could give him a ride on the air.

If these fellows is swept away by the wind, the first fellow will certainly be screaming his life out in fear till he lands, while the second fellow will be having a time of his life smiling till he lands. Even if the wind lands them in the mud, the first fellow would still be crying home while the second fellow smiles back home, hoping to get such an experience again.

The reason many people cry over certain situations is also because they refuse to see differently. We must also get to see from the eyes of God, what He intends to achieve with every situation in our lives.

CHAPTER SEVEN

GO FOR THEM

CHAPTER SEVEN

GO FOR THEM

For what God intends to make out many lives, we see that there is first a need for gathering, and proper following that the life of Jesus be formed in the lives of men and their lives used for mighty works, to the glory of our God.

It seems we are tired already, but rather what I see now is a bid for church growth without evangelism. I see a bid for numbers but counting off those that should actually be in the numbers.

So many are yearning in their hearts that their lives can have a meaning but they need to be shown the way, so many are longing for peace of mind, and they have sought for it in all places they could but cannot find it. If only they knew someone who could point them to the price of peace.

Some are in despair and looking for someone who can share in their burden but if only there is someone out there, could direct them to Him who says, *"Come all ye that are heavy laden and I will give you rest"*.

They try to build up their physique, raise their heads high and walk with a smile. They seem strong headed and stable but deep within that person is an emptiness that is longing to be filled.

While on this work, someone sent an article to me, which made me begin to wonder, is the church to be blamed? Have we really done and are we still doing what we were called to do which is the reconciliation of men to God.

THE UNPREACHED GOSPEL

You heard he is a cultist. You could not believe it rather you said, "He is so young and just 16 years, in ss1". Now you have seen him with marijuana parting his lips, a tattooed snake on his arm and in his hands is a bottle of beer. You heard him say that his favourite date is the 7th of July and you assumed that was his birthday.

You stood and criticized him, you told your friends that hell awaits him as you shook your head and said to yourself "he is already doomed" but you do not know that within the bad hard guy lies a fragile aching heart wanting to be loved and showed a little care. Now he finds solace in his gang because his dad and mom are on the brink of divorce.

She knocked on your door asking to help you do anything for food and money. She looked so unkempt and malnourished, you were torn between pity and disbelief. You know her uncle to be a rich and religious man, an elder in his church, and you cannot help but wonder why she would be in this sorry state. You concluded that she has been wayward and disrespectful and this is his way of punishing her for some time. Without asking her any questions, you managed to give her a rumpled 100 naira note and sent her away telling her never to come back. She leaves fighting tears, wondering how she would go back to her uncle who had sworn not to take care of her except she warms his bed.

That man you saw yesterday has been going through a hard time. He is a job-hunting father who just lost his only son and has been pondering on how to bury his dead son. He bumped into you and before he could apologize, you have rained insults on him. You saw the tears well up in his eyes but you did not bother to show any empathy. To you, he is just a depressed fellow who should not bother others with his worries.

You saw her in a bar, wrecking of alcohol. She kept laughing and muttering to herself, "why? Why?" you walked past her, even though a voice inside of you kept telling you to find out her problem. You shut the voice down and tagged her "A cheap drunk" but that cheap drunk is a widow who had just been diagnosed with breast cancer, moreover she just lost her job a month ago. Now, she thinks those bottles of alcohol could wash away her sorrow. And you claim to have the light, you boast with the scriptures because you know only the letters but devoid of revelation.

I began to wonder why Jesus didn't choose the Pharisees', the Sadducee's and the scribes as his disciples seeing that this people already know and teach the scriptures, since these men were probably just the most qualified for the work. What did he actually need a fisherman for? Of what good was a tax collector in this ministerial calling?

But yet, it is just so surprising that those were the caliber of people Jesus decided to choose. Men without any spiritual or ministerial background per se.

Again I began I wonder, why didn't Jesus die in between two candles in the temple, rather he chose to die in between two thieves at Calvary.

Have we as the church not enveloped the message of the gospel in the confines of the church wall. We expect them to come to church and get the word, but we fail to recognize that the church is not even in the agenda of these men.

We have closed them out, we have already condemned them in our hearts, we use them to preach our messages but yet I feel the Lord is hurt with our traditions.

UNNOTICED BIAS

We have only sought to visit only our regular members in our visitations, we see the rest as non-serious Christians, and the devil is maximizing the opportunities we are missing. He goes out for them, captures their hearts and uses them, because whichever way, every man is tagged "WANTED".

Even as I write this, yet my own heart is heavy as I am also guilty. We think that they are of no use to the kingdom, but these are a set that the Lord desires to use to turn this world around. Men He can gather, to work on their lives and use them for a holy uproar.

Broken men who won't fear the arrows of the devil anymore, men who will face the devil with a holy anger in their eyes because of the number of their wasted years, and men who will face the devil head on, leaving no stone unturned in the city.

But intentionally or unintentionally, we have shut the doors of the gospel on them and it grieves the Lord.

They seem worthless but we must show them the great worth, God had placed in them. They seem useless but we must show them, how mighty the works God can use them to accomplish. They seem inconsequential, but in those little things lies great abilities.

Where is that hunger for souls that burned in the hearts of our fathers? Where is the Love our fathers showed, that transformed the lives of broken men and gave their lives a meaning? Were we not called to be the salt of the earth, that we might give the lives of men taste? Were we not called to be the light of the world, that we might shine our lights into the dark lives of men that they may find their way?

We have become so concerned with our religious activities that we have neglected the men on the streets who need to come to Christ and yet we try to justify our acts with the scriptures "Doesn't the bible say."

Doesn't the bible say in 2 Corinthians 6:14 *"Be ye not unequally yoked together with unbelievers: for what fellowship hath righteousness with unrighteousness? And what communion hath light with darkness?"* Have become our anthem and our excuse but doesn't the bible say too that he desires that no soul may perish.

"The Lord is not being slow in doing what he promised —the way some people understand slowness. But God is being patient with you. He doesn't want anyone to be lost. He wants everyone to change their ways and stop sinning." – 2 Peter 3:9

We think that smoker hidden in that dark corner does not care about Jesus, but he is right there trying to forget his misery through the smokes which does not even take the misery away.

What have we done that the Lord may be glorified in his life? We hiss even when we pass him blowing his smoke to the air, and we condemn him in our hearts but we never made a move towards the salvation of his soul. A worth full soul turned worthless.

JESUS, THE DIFFERENCE

I plead the Lord to have mercy on my life because I am also guilty of these issues He will be raising up. There are people whose lives could have been a mess if Jesus didn't come their way. Many of us whose lives would have made no meaning until Jesus came knocking on our doors.

Peter would have lived his whole life and died as a fisherman if Jesus didn't come his way. Zaccheaus would have lived his whole life as a sinful tax collector if Christ had not appeared, Mary Magdalene would have wasted her life as a prostitute if Jesus didn't come her way.

We must remember that as lights that we are, God lights us up with the life of Jesus and places us to shine so that others may be see the light and walk aright. The presence of Christ, makes the whole difference in anybody's life. His presence turned the life patterns of these souls and set their lives on the right track.

And daily we profess, we carry Jesus in our lives and I simply ask, how many souls has the Christ in our lives transformed to the right path? Have we not missed it even as a church?

I read a story of a young lady, her parents were divorced and she had gotten in drugs at an early age. She was constantly having issues at work, have been severally sexually abused, she sought for where to find peace. She had no friend except her box of cigarettes, and she was thinking of ending her life.

One day she came and sat in front of the church in her neighborhood, feeling this urge to go inside if this Christ she has always heard about would meet her and grant her peace.

She sat for long as she watched people troop in, certainly the service has started as she could hear songs from the church building.

Quietly she walked into the church and sat at the back. Of course she was badly dressed with her tattered jeans trouser and her hair she had given different colours.

She came to seek solace, but the piercing looks of people on her with disgust shattered her heart the more. Sitting right there, she made up her mind to commit suicide as soon she leaves.

As soon as service was over, she saw people walking out, some in groups exchanging pleasantries, some walked past her still with that look of disgust, I can imagine what was going through their minds, "Hamm, what has this one come to do in church? Does this place look like a party ground?"

I can imagine the thoughts of disgust going through their minds "uhhhh, just look out how this girl dressed to church with tattered jeans and even painted her hair, oh God have mercy" but no one said a word to her.

She walked out of the church more broken than she came, just for a woman to tap her back and ask how she was doing and that she must be a first timer as she haven't seen her in church before. And that was just the beginning of how a broken lady who would have committed suicide came to the knowledge of Christ.

Becoming born again, she decided to go for broken ladies, having a clear understanding of what they are going through, based on the experience of what she passed through, she knew just how to relate with them, and what they actually needed. That's exactly what I call a *"worm turned into a threshing instrument". Worthless turned mighty.*

The story depicts the way the church drives away people whom the Lord brought to them, rather than the church being a place of solace and refuge, we tell them Christ hates sinners rather than tell them the truth of God's love for sinners and his hate for sin.

CHAPTER EIGHT

POWER OF INSIGNIFICANT THINGS

CHAPTER EIGHT

POWER OF INSIGNIFICANT THINGS

Just like there is value and worth in the things we term "worthless", so is there great might and power in the terms we term "Insignificant". One mystery people have refused to accept is that little or small things are usually the most powerful. One of the scriptures that marvel me a great deal when it comes to insignificance or little is Zechariah 4:10.

"For who has despised the time of insignificant things? They will rejoice to see the plumb line in the hand of Zerubbabel..." – Zechariah 4:10 (ISV)

"Those who have made fun of this day of small beginnings will celebrate when they see Zerubbabel holding this important stone..." (CEV)

"Everyone should know that the day of small things are important..." (Easy English)

One would naturally assume little things to be things that should be despised, ignored, looked down on and possibly made fun of. Little things which we would consider not to matter. So many places in the bible, it mentions about the power of these little things.

Things we may think makes no difference, INSIGNIFICANT as it sounds. But if the bible is saying that we should not despise them, it means there is a SIGNIFICANCE in that INSIGNIFICANCE. Just like people would say in every NONSENSE there is a SENSE and just as we have also seen in the previous chapters of this book that even in the things we term WORTHLESS, there is a great WORTH.

No matter how much we despise, overlook or look down on little things, the power they exhibit cannot be denied of them. As small as my heart is, if it stops functioning, even my big skull will collapse.

As big as a ship is, that it requires strong winds to drive them yet it is directed by just a small steer or rudder, as big as a horse is, yet it is directed by a little bridle in its mouth bringing it to obey its master, as big as our body is, yet it can be set on fire by its little member, the tongue.

As big as an elephant is, it has not killed as much that little mosquito has and as big as a mosquito is, yet it has never held the world to ransom as the little corona virus we don't see has. Little things have power.

TIME OF SMALL BEGINNING

The little beginning of a man is as powerful if not even more powerful than the end. The phase of the beginning is a period of capacity building. The phase of little beginning is the period of root deepening.

You must start off small, get well rooted and then blossom. Even if others laugh at you now, don't laugh at yourself too by quitting. Don't despise your little start, for there you may learn what will keep you when you finally get to the top.

THE MUSTARD SEED

Then Jesus told the people another story: "God's kingdom is like a mustard seed that a man plants in his field. It is the smallest of all seeds but when it grows it is the largest of all garden plants. It becomes a tree big enough for the birds to come and make nests in its branches – Math 13:31 (ISV)

I love this scripture so much in regards to little things that I love breaking it down into smaller churns to discuss, that we may get a fuller package of God's thoughts towards little things.

God's kingdom is like a mustard seed . As mighty and powerful the kingdom of God is, yet it was likened to a seed, not just a seed but the smallest of all seeds. Another thing that should never be despised are seeds. So many have missed big blessings because it came in small packages. Ladies have lost mighty men because as at the time of their meeting, they looked poor (small).

I love the story of the man who tried giving his son a sports car that he was always yearning for but wrapped the key in a bible. The package didn't come as expected hence the boy despised the gift and cut off all communication with his father only to come after his fathers' death to discover the key of the sports car he always dreamed of, was in the bible his dad gave him years ago.

Your breakthrough may be in that business idea, you are despising because it looks little, it can be that work you despise because the salary is little, and it can be anything but today you must recognize that little things are powerful. Great things most times, come in little packages.

That a man plants in his field. There are two things, one can possibly do with his seeds. He can either choose to eat them or he chooses to plant them. You eat your seeds, then get ready to stay hungry without hopes of another meal but plant your seeds and you can have hope for food tomorrow. Jesus said except a seed is corn is thrown into the ground and dies, it cannot bear fruits.

As powerful as seeds are, yet the power can never be unleashed until they are planted. That idea cannot grow until you plant it, that song cannot be heard over the nations until it has been sung, that book cannot touch lives across cities and nations until it is written. You must put to work what God have placed in your hands.

It is the smallest of all seeds. Having said that great things most times come in little packages, we should hence, know the need of not despising even the smallest of things. Don't be scared of starting that business idea even with just one dollar. I once read that the UPS delivery company was started by two teenagers with only a bicycle and a borrowed $100. They started from a basement but today UPS delivers 20 million packages every day and is worth $100 billion.

But when it grows. The word "When" denotes time. Your seed may be viable and you may have planted but you must also give it time. This draws my mind back to the time of little beginning.

Imagine someone showing you a mustard tree in its mightiness, gives you the seed and then says to you, "plant and tend to this tiny seed and soon you will have this mighty tree". You obey the command, planted and you tended to it and in a few months' time, you are disappointed at the size already. In your heart, this is not the tree the man promised you and in anger you uproot the little plant.

So many have given up on ideas that could have announced them to the world because they gave up and despised the time of their little beginning. There is power in your seed but you must give it time.

It is the largest of all garden plants. This shows us the capacity of little to become great. Don't be scared of starting that business even though with a dollar, because a viable seed has the capacity to grow. Don't be scared to establish that idea though it be little, because with time it has capacity to become great and soon you can say like Jacob did in Gen 30:30 *"For it was **little** which thou hadst before I came, and it is now **increased unto a multitude** and the Lord hath blessed thee…;* that the little which you had is increased unto a multitude.

And this brings us to a very sensitive aspect of your seeds which we must not neglect. In your planting, be careful of the labourers you choose to tend to your seeds. Laban's house experienced exponential growth because a Jacob was working there. Hence if you wouldn't despise your little seed, and not be scared of planting but give it time, God is willing to bless it and increase it.

It becomes a tree big enough for the birds to come and make nests in its branches. The power of a seed to grow into a mighty tree is not just for itself but for others. This part of this scripture is very vital in the power of insignificant things. True power lies in kingdom and societal relevance.

When God establishes you, He expects that other find theirs through you and that's why Jesus also told peter "When thou art strengthened, strengthen thy brothers'. Kingdom relevance is also exemplified by societal relevance.

LEARN TO WAIT

Another scripture, God have always used to amplify the secret of the mustard seed is found in Isaiah 60:22

The smallest family will become a large family group. The smallest tribe will become a powerful nation. WHEN THE TIME IS RIGHT, I, the LORD, will come quickly. I will make these things happen." – Isaiah 60:22 (ISV)

The scripture clearly states it here, the smallest family will become a large family group, and the smallest tribe will become a powerful nation just as we see the mustard seed to be the smallest of seeds but can become the largest of all garden plants.

Again we see in Isaiah 60:22 that God will do this only when the time is right. We cannot rush him in our making, hence waiting becomes an unavoidable factor.

Steve Harvey said in one of his telecasts *"when a Christian asks God for something, God packs it up and sends to the Christian but what God doesn't promise the Christian is the time, his package will arrive".*

In as much as God wants to see you have every single thing, you are asking of Him right now, but He will not be insensitive to give them to you at the wrong time. No matter how much a fourteen year old boy cries to be given the car keys, even if you have taught him to drive, you still would not hand those keys over to him because he is crying for them. Even if you are sure, he will not crash into someone but you certainly know he will get arrested, he has to wait the next four years if that's what it would take for him to be matured enough to drive out by himself.

That little dream can turn out to a mighty reality, but can you wait till the time is right? Your song can be the best selling in 2023 but if released in 2022, no matter how beautiful it is, may not sell a copy.

JUST A LITTLE

Your proud talk is not good. You know the saying, "Just a little yeast makes the whole batch of dough rise: – 1 Cor 5:6 (ISV)

Beautiful things that can build up are small, in the same way things that can bring down. Just a little yeast can make the whole batch to rise, and scripture also speaks of little foxes that spoil the vine.

Certain character flaws that we seem to overlook, but gradually, they are eating into and eating up destinies.

The enemy will never place an attack over your destiny with "big temptations" because he knows you will discover it and put up a resistance. He will rather choose to send his great army one after another, until he has raised an army big enough within your courts to pull down your city gates and destroy it to ruins.

The statement *"just a little"* have destroyed many and is still destroying many because we have refused to acknowledge the power that lies in little. Many have turned drunkards simply because they wanted to taste 'a little', some have become addicts to one habit or another by wanting *'a little'*.

'Just a little' engages our minds into character flaws we don't seem to even notice, and some other times, we notice but yet too small to us that we should bother. See how message bible puts 1 Corinthians 5:6.

"Your flip and callous arrogance in these things bothers me. You pass it off as a small thing, but it's anything but that. Yeast, too is a "small thing," but it works its way through a whole batch of bread dough pretty fast" – 1 Cor 5:6 (MSG)

From that scripture we see "Yeast too is a small thing **but**"…, that pride is a small thing **but**…, we understand that your arrogance is quite small **but**…, I agree with you that this anger issue is the best we can get of you **but**…, your own lust is even small compared to youths of your age, that's ok **but**…, there are so many of these issues which so many of us have overlooked and have closed our eyes to the after effects.

How I wish there were no after effects, but unfortunately we cannot run away from the after effects which is the destruction that lies ahead. Solomon in his Songs calls them *little foxes* that spoil the vine and in Ecclesiastes, calls them *a few dead flies*. They are little but powerful enough to render a vine useless. They are few yet can spoil the sweet fragrance that God intends your life to produce.

A few dead flies will make even the best perfume

*stink. In the same way, "a little" foolishness can
ruin much wisdom and honor. – Eccl 10:1 (ESV)*

*Catch the foxes, the little foxes, before they ruin
our vineyard in bloom. – SOS 2:15 (GNB)*

As mighty and powerful wisdom is, yet when much wisdom comes face to face with just a little foolishness, wisdom can be brought to ruins.

The foxes are quite little but they are powerful enough to render a vine useless and this is the more reason why we must kill these foxes here before they spoil our vine.

We must bare ourselves to the double edged sword of God's word. Jesus can help us clean these dead flies that wants to overshadow the fragrance of our lives. He told his disciples, you are clean by the words that I speak to you (John 15:3).

Hence we have so overlooked so many things because we thought them to be little, not knowing the great power they possess. It may be a habit which we call insignificant but the devil is looking for any loophole it can get and would be grateful for any space, no matter how small.

James 3:5 tells us of a little flame that can bring down a thick forest. It doesn't matter how many trees may be in it, actually just a spark as the CEV bible puts it can make it look like there was never a single tree existing there.

---

*...Just think how large a forest can be set on
fire by a tiny flame! - James 3:5 (GNB)*

The devil will never fight you in growing a name for yourself as long as he knows that you are not growing integrity with it.

The enemy does not mind, you having multitudes following you when he knows you have not gathered strength just withstand public opinion. Just a little persecution he may set up, can destroy a ministry of many years. Just a little disagreement he can spark up, may bring crumbling that career you have strived so hard to build for years.

USE YOUR LITTLE

Having understood that there is nothing God cannot use to make a difference in this world no matter how little, we must also come to a point where we are conscious enough to release our little to be used of God.

Your little words can encourage a weary soul, it can strengthen feeble knees, and it can save a dying soul. Your little smile can put a smile in another's face. You can never imagine how much God can do with your little if handed over to Him.

The little boy who brought his five loaves of bread and two fishes could never have imagined his little could be used to feed so great a crowd as 5000 men.

When the Lord began to ask Moses, what was in his hands, Moses may have been thinking of what use a staff is, to this host of armies facing us. So many a times, we seem to neglect or misappropriate our authorities simply because the instrument seemed little or insignificant.

Just as the worth of a man is dependent on whom He is working for, so is the significance of a thing dependent on whose hands it is. A jaw bone would be so useless and insignificant in times of battle to any other Israelites but in the hands of Samson, it was a powerful armor.

www.ingramcontent.com/pod-product-compliance
Lightning Source LLC
Chambersburg PA
CBHW072105150726
47999CB00005B/1896